PAST-LIFE REGRESSION

URSULA MARKHAM holds a diploma in hypnotherapy and has been practising Past-Life Regression since 1982. She has trained others in the same field since 1985 and has lectured widely on the subject both in the UK and the USA. Ursula runs business training seminars for companies in stress management, works as a counsellor and is the author of numerous books on a wide range of issues concerning personal growth and well-being, from bereavement to self-hypnosis, childhood trauma and miscarriage.

Selected Vega titles by the same author

The Beginner's Guide To Self-Hypnosis
Bereavement (Vega Guides Series)
Creating A Positive Self-Image
Ultimate Stress Handbook For Women
Women Under Pressure
Managing Stress

PAST-LIFE REGRESSION

HOW TO LEARN FROM THE LIVES YOU HAVE LIVED

URSULA MARKHAM

ISBN 1-84333-741-X

A catalogue record for this book is available from the British Library

Published in 2003 by Vega, The Chrysalis Building, Bramley Road, London, W10 6SP

An imprint of **Chrysalis** Books Group plc

Visit our website at www.chrysalisbooks.co.uk

Jacket design: Roland Codd
Editor: Richard Emerson
Managing Editor: Laurence Henderson
Production: Kate Rogers
Printed in Great Britain
by Creative Print and Design, Wales

To all those people who mean so much to me today – and probably always have.

'Learning is finding out what you already know.
Doing is demonstrating that you know it.'
Richard Bach, Illusions

CONTENTS

INTRODUCTION

When I first began working as a hypnotherapist, over twenty years ago, most of those who came to see me were interested in problems such as losing weight, giving up smoking or dealing with relatively minor habits, like nail-biting. How things have changed. The smokers and those who are overweight still exist, of course, but most of my patients are seeking methods of dealing with far more deep-rooted problems that, although they may have some sort of physical manifestation, have actually been caused by some earlier traumatic life experience.

Those problems may be as varied as phobias, fear of relationships, lack of confidence, debilitating stammer, insomnia or feelings of inadequacy. But there is one fact that is common to all – if the patients are to be helped to overcome their problems and to go on to live fulfilling and happy lives, they need to acknowledge and understand the causes of their present condition. The easiest and most painless way of doing this is by means of hypnotic regression.

This regression is, of course, only the first step on the path to true self-awareness; it is not an ultimate cure in itself. But that first step is the most important one of all. Without it, whatever treatment the individual may receive – whether by hypnosis or some other means – would do little more than superimpose an artificial veneer of self-confidence over a troubled inner self. This would lead to more problems in the future, when the experiences of the past discovered a new way of invading the present. It is rather like putting a piece of sticking plaster over an open wound without first bothering to clean or treat the wound itself. You might not be able to see it festering away beneath the dressing, but you can be certain that it is doing so and that it could go on to cause more serious – and certainly more painful – problems in the future. In addition, the majority of people find that it helps them to know and understand the reason for their symptoms. Sometimes that need may be on a subconscious level and, if the basic cause were not discovered, the consequence would be the emergence of a new set of symptoms at a later date.

Individuals have their own subconscious 'filing system' where everything ever seen, heard or learned is permanently stored. Just as with a real filing system, a good deal of what is there is not really needed and so it is relegated to the backs of drawers and cupboards to lie there and gather dust. Through hypnosis, however, it is possible to search through that filing system in order to find any relevant piece of information that the mind might require – although one may well be looking at it from a viewpoint that is very different from the one that existed when that information was first stored there.

Imagine what it would be like if you were suddenly to come across a diary that you had kept when you were sixteen years old. The words would describe the feelings and emotions of someone of sixteen with all the problems, hopes and fears experienced at that age. Looking at that diary perhaps some twenty years later, you might smile at how insurmountable some of those problems had seemed to you at the time – and how you wish they were all that you had to worry about today! But that does not mean that, to the sixteen-year-old, those problems were not very real indeed. The effect of those problems on his or her life was very real too.

Regression is rather like that. Reliving and re-experiencing a situation through hypnosis is not intended to make you forget past events or pretend that they did not happen. It is just meant to help you put them into perspective and see that something that may have had a devastating effect upon you when you were ten years old (and continued to do so thereafter) has a far less devastating effect when viewed through the eyes of, say, a forty-year-old.

The value of using hypnotic regression in the treatment of a problem – and remember that regression only constitutes one part of the treatment, the ensuing therapy being the other – is that the patient will not get rid of one set of symptoms only to replace them with another. This is because they have been able to go back and see for themselves, hopefully with mature understanding, the original cause of the problem; once they have dealt with that original cause, it no longer needs to have any effect on their present life.

There are two types of regression. The first is regression to earlier stages in the patient's present life, and the second is regression to a possible former life. The actual existence of past lives will be discussed later in this book, but the therapy is equally effective whether one believes that reincarnation is possible or that the facts revealed are simply a product of the patient's subconscious mind.

As will be indicated in Chapter One, hypnosis is not the only available method of inducing regression – but it is the only one I use. Apart from the fact that I have been a practising hypnotherapist for many years, I truly believe that it is the speediest, the most effective and the least painful way of achieving positive results. So it is only regression therapy by means of hypnosis that I shall be discussing in this book. I hope that, by the time you reach the final page, you will be as confident as I am in the technique itself and in its therapeutic value as an improver of lives.

[1]

THE BACKGROUND
TO HYPNOSIS

Hypnosis has been around for a long, long time. No one really knows its origins but it was certainly used therapeutically by the Ancient Egyptians, Greeks and Romans. Since that time it has had a somewhat chequered history – at certain times being in favour and at others being disapproved of most heartily. The ancient civilizations were firm believers in a form of hypnosis (the word itself had not been coined at that time, only coming into existence in the early nineteenth century – it derives from the Greek word hypnos, meaning 'sleep').

As time went on, however, its curative uses came to be regarded with increasing suspicion, an attitude not assisted by novels such as Trilby (1894) by George du Maurier. This was the tale of an artist's model, Trilby, who came under the 'mesmeric' control of a musician, Svengali. This best-selling story helped convince an already sceptical public that to submit to hypnosis was to give up all free will and to place one's mind in the power of another.

PIONEERS OF HYPNOSIS

One name associated with hypnotism that is probably known to most people is that of the eighteenth-century physician Anton Mesmer, yet what Mesmer did was not really hypnosis at all. Having undergone training as a priest, Mesmer then studied law before finally turning to medicine. It was his belief that magnetism would provide a cure for many ailments. He used to attach magnets to the bodies of his patients and did, in fact, achieve many recorded 'cures' – although whether these recoveries were brought about by the magnets or by the sheer charisma of the man himself is uncertain. Mesmer came to Paris under the patronage of the court of Louis XVI, and was soon called upon to treat those in high society. He was a great showman who liked to set the scene for his work – dimming lights, perfuming the air with incense and employing strange music. He would wave his arms in the air, telling his patients they were receiving 'magnetic fluid' that was going to cure them.

In 1778, a commission set up to investigate Mesmer condemned his activities. He was forced to retire and went to Meersburg where he spent the remainder of his life. He left behind him a number of followers – and, of course, the word 'mesmerism', which is still in use today.

Another pioneer was the Marquis de Puységur, a disciple of Mesmer. The Marquis was treating a farm labourer for a chest complaint by following his master's technique of waving his hands in the air when the man passed into a state called at the time 'magnetic somnambulism'. In effect, he exhibited all the classic signs of having been hypnotized.

Dr John Elliotson, a nineteenth-century Professor of Medicine at University College, London and President of the Royal Medical Society, used hypnosis when treating his patients. While at University College, he was said to have performed painless surgery using hypnosis, but in 1838 the hospital's council passed a resolution forbidding this practice. However, as he was a well-respected man, Elliotson was able to promote the concept of hypnosis as a genuine form of treatment.

Dr James Braid, who originally coined the word 'hypnotism', was the first to prove that hypnosis could be achieved without the use of magnets, and a Scottish doctor, James Esdaile, spent much of his life in India performing many operations using what he called 'mesmeric anaesthesia'.

A well-respected nineteenth-century French professor, Jean-Martin Charcot, was responsible for founding the Salpetriere School of Hypnotism in France and for bringing credibility to the subject. Professor Charcot, along with professors at the University of Nancy, were convinced that hypnosis could be induced satisfactorily by correct verbal suggestion. These were distinguished men, respected in their profession, so it was no longer possible to claim that hypnosis was something used only by cranks and eccentrics.

PIONEERS OF HYPNOTIC REGRESSION

It was not until the work of Pierre Janet, another nineteenth-century pioneer, that anyone began to consider the subject of regression. During the course of his work, Janet, who was a pupil of Charcot, found that patients suffering from what he termed 'neurotic disorders' often had significant gaps in their long-term memories — they had managed to block out incidents from long ago that had been particularly painful or excessively distressing. Using hypnosis, Janet was able to help his patients recall those past events. Such recall led these individuals to a deeper understanding of themselves and of the traumatic effect on their life of the hitherto 'forgotten' incidents.

Understanding, of course, is the essential first step on the path to a cure. It is not a painful experience provided the patient is being treated by a trained and ethical therapist who will also give the kind of follow-up treatment described in the case histories contained in later chapters of this book.

The somewhat better-known Sigmund Freud, the pioneer of psychoanalysis, worked with Janet at one time. It was Freud who made the first extensive use of hypnosis to probe the depths of the subconscious mind. He was also one of the first to insist that the discovery of the root cause of a problem is an essential first stage in achieving a cure. Freud's difficulties arose from the fact that he did not fully appreciate the need for co-operation between patient and therapist; he was inclined to treat his patients as docile subjects with little or no role to play in their own treatment. As a consequence of this approach, he often failed to bring about cures and subsequently became disillusioned with hypnosis as a form of therapy. Today, of course, it is recognized that no real success can be achieved by a therapist working alone and that the patient's full co-operation is essential.

REGRESSION GAINS ACCEPTANCE

During the first part of the twentieth century, after the time of Pierre Janet and Sigmund Freud, little consideration was given to the subject of regression. As time went on and hypnosis gained credibility and was thought of as more than just a form of stage entertainment, more and more hypnotherapists began to use present life regression in their work. But the whole concept of past-life regression was thought to be at best unbelievable and, at worst, a case of dabbling in an area that was better left unexplored. Then came two men (to be followed by others) who made very significant contributions to the area of past-life regression. One was Morey Bernstein, who worked in the United States, and the other was Arnall Bloxham, who worked in Britain.

MOREY BERNSTEIN

Morey Bernstein was a hypnotherapist of repute in the United States. In the beginning, he was very sceptical about the concept of past-life regression and only ventured into the field almost by accident. As a hypnotherapist, Bernstein had been consulted by, and had successfully treated, a Colorado woman called Virginia Tighe. In the course of her treatment, Bernstein regressed Mrs Tighe, intending to take her back to an earlier time in her current life. But, during treatment, she claimed that she was able to remember a previous incarnation when she had lived in Ireland and had had the name Bridey Murphy.

BRIDEY'S STORY

As described in trance by Virginia Tighe, Bridey Murphy was born in Cork in 1798. She was the daughter of Duncan Murphy and his wife Kathleen and she had a brother, also called Duncan. Bridey attended a school run by a woman called Mrs Strayne, whose daughter was later to become the wife of Duncan Junior. When Bridey was twenty years old, she married Sean McCarthy, the Protestant son of a local barrister. The couple went to live in Belfast where Bridey's husband taught law at Queen's University. They remained childless. Bridey died at the age of sixty-six.

THE PROOF

Although Virginia Tighe had never been to Ireland in her current life, as Bridey Murphy she was able to give many names and details that were later verified. These names included those of two Belfast grocers, from whom she purchased provisions, as well as details of a tobacco house and a rope company operating in Belfast at that time.

Even those facts that were initially refuted by experts later turned out to be true. For example, Bridey claimed to have been punished when she scraped the paint off her metal bed. At first experts insisted that iron beds did not appear in Ireland until the mid-nineteenth century. But it was later proved that such beds had been imported there a hundred years earlier. Bridey mentioned reading a book called 'The Sorrows of Deirdre' and experts claimed that, according to their records, this book did not appear until 1905. It was later discovered that a book entitled The Song of Deirdre was published in 1808.

During these regressions, Bridey Murphy spoke in a voice that Bernstein described as 'a weary half-whine with a throaty Irish accent'. This was not the accent typically used by actors when portraying Irish people and was, in fact, a localized form of speech. Not only would Mrs Tighe not have known about the accent in the first place, she would have had to have been a brilliant actress to fake it and to sustain it throughout each of the six sessions of regression.

Morey Bernstein regressed Virginia Tighe to the lifetime of Bridey Murphy some six times in all, between late 1952 and mid 1953. He had chosen her as his subject not only because of her initial spontaneous regression to a previous life but also because she was a subject who automatically went into the deep-trance state. Bernstein went on to use recordings of those six sessions of regression as the basis of a book he published in 1956, which he called The Search for Bridey Murphy. In this book, Bernstein gave Virginia Tighe the pseudonym 'Ruth Simmons'.

ARNALL BLOXHAM

Arnall Bloxham was a Cardiff-based hypnotherapist with a great interest in the concept of reincarnation. From childhood, he had been convinced that he had lived before and this belief never left him. Over a period of about twenty years, from the mid-1950s, Arnall Bloxham conducted many sessions of hypnotic past-life regression. He recorded many of these – collectively known as The Bloxham Tapes. Although some of the detailed information contained on those tapes may seem comparatively uninteresting, the fact that they appear to refer to the previous lives of the subjects is fascinating in itself. Also contained on those tapes are facts that experts have accepted as little known and yet absolutely correct, leading to the belief by many that the regressions were indeed genuine. Television producer Jeffrey Iverson was sufficiently interested to write a book about Bloxham's experiments and a documentary film was made based on the tapes and the material they contained. Bloxham's first subject was a schoolteacher by the name of Ann Ockenden who, under hypnosis, was able to describe seven previous lives.

THE CASE OF JANE EVANS

Another of Bloxham's subjects was Jane Evans, who was regressed to six previous lives in all. She was able to describe one previous existence as Rebecca, a young Jewish woman living in York, England, who had died a violent death during a massacre of the Jews in 1190. The facts related by Jane Evans during this regression were confirmed as accurate by Professor Barrie Dobson, an expert on the York massacres.

THE CASE OF GRAHAM HUXTABLE

Welshman Graham Huxtable regressed to a life as a gunner's mate on a ship engaged in the blockade of the coast of France during the Napoleonic Wars. He gave a dramatic account of a battle with a ship of the French fleet and was to relate details of practices on board ship that had long since ceased. He also used the colloquial language of the day. Earl Louis Mountbatten (of Burma) was so fascinated by the wealth of detail that Huxtable was able to give about naval life of the period that he borrowed the tapes and played them to experts in naval history.

Huxtable also told how a blast of cannon fire had shot his leg away and vividly described the agony this had caused. It is worth mentioning here a fact that will be explained in more detail later in this book. It is now possible for someone to be regressed to a time of great pain in a former life without having to re-experience the pain itself. But this was not the case in Bloxham's day. This is not to imply any criticism of Arnall Bloxham, who was at the forefront of experimental work in past-life regression when modern techniques had not yet been developed.

EDGAR CAYCE

Edgar Cayce is perhaps best known as one of the most famous of the American psychic healers but he was also extremely interested in the concept of reincarnation and in exploring past lives. Cayce's interest in hypnosis came about because, when he was twenty-four years old, he had a throat ailment that resulted in him completely losing his voice. Desperate to find help, he consulted hypnotherapist Al Layne – but this was no ordinary session of hypnosis. Once in the hypnotic trance, Edgar Cayce was not only able to speak but also prescribed a cure for his own condition – a treatment that subsequently proved to be successful. From that time on, he was able to prescribe for other people by entering the trance state and allowing the cures to 'come into his mind'.

PAST-LIFE CURES

In 1923, Cayce began to speak, when in trance, of the past lives of the people seeking his help. After that, whenever he was asked to provide a cure for someone's condition, he would automatically look at their previous incarnations for a solution. An organization called The Association for Research and Enlightenment (ARE) still exists in Virginia Beach, USA as a memorial to the work of Edgar Cayce. It holds transcripts of his readings and has many associated study groups.

DR IAN STEVENSON

Dr Ian Stevenson, a Canadian, was professor of psychiatry and director of the Department of Parapsychology at the University of Virginia, Charlottesville. He also undertook probably the most detailed research and academic study of reincarnation and past-life regression. Dr Stevenson and his colleagues collected an international census of cases of regression from all over the world. These were collated, examined and analysed in as much detail as possible. He went on to publish a scholarly work based on these investigations. Much of Dr

Stevenson's work was carried out in the Indian sub-continent and, in contrast to other researchers, he did a great deal of work with very young children in that area.

THE CASE OF IMAD ELAWAR

Imad Elawar was born in the Lebanese village of Kornayei in 1958. Nine years earlier, a man called Ibrahim Bouhamzy had died in the village of Khriby, about thirty miles away. From the age of two, Imad would talk about the time when he had lived in Khriby, giving names and details of people he knew and places he had visited. Dr Stevenson, whose contact with Imad began when the boy was about five years old, reported that the way Imad described these experiences was unlike the 'storytelling' of a small child.

Imad was able to give personal details of family and friends and their relationships with each other. He also spoke about a mistress whom he had loved but whom he had not been able to marry because she was of a lower caste. Dr Stevenson called this woman Jamileh. He also interviewed more than twenty relatives and friends of both Ibrahim and Imad and visited both villages on several occasions. On one occasion, Imad accompanied Dr Stevenson on a visit to Ibrahim's village and, during the car journey, told him of fifty-seven items that he could remember. He was correct in fifty-one cases and it was thought that the few mistakes he had made were due to confusion in the small boy's mind between his present and past lives. Ian Stevenson was also responsible for scrutinizing the evidence produced in other cases of past-life regression.

THE CASE OF JOANNE MACIVER

Joanne MacIver was hypnotized by her father, Ken MacIver, and regressed to various other lives. During one of these regressions she claimed to be a woman called Susan Ganier, who had lived on a farm in Canada. As Susan, Joanne was able to describe names and places that were later found to have existed, although they had long since disappeared from most records and maps.

THE CASE OF EDWARD RYALL

Edward Ryall was born in England in 1902 and had felt from early childhood that he had lived before. When Edward was just eight years old, his father took him out into the garden to show him Halley's comet. Edward told his father that he had seen it before – which, of course, his father did not believe. In a later regression, Edward told of the time he had shown the comet to his own son. The year was 1682.

Dr Stevenson was interested in Edward Ryall's case and went on to write an introduction to the book, Second Time Around, that Ryall wrote about his life as John Fletcher. Fletcher was a farmer who died in a skirmish just prior to the Battle of Sedgemoor, when the Duke of Monmouth's forces were defeated by the men of James II. Edward Ryall's book contains facts that only those who had studied the period concerned could know. He knew words and phrases no longer in use and could describe in detail the workings of agricultural implements of the time. He also made a detailed sketch of the route taken by the Duke of Monmouth's army – a route known only to those who were expert in that period of history.

DR STEVENSON'S OPINIONS

Dr Stevenson is very fair in his analysis of these memories of former lives. He does not insist that each of them was an example of past-life regression – although he does not imply any fraud on the part of the people concerned. In some cases he feels that knowledge was possibly acquired at some time and later forgotten by the conscious mind of the subject. However, as he points out, this does not explain how little children, as yet unable to read or to travel alone, were able to give such clear details of their previous lives.

THE PRESENT DAY

Today David Canova, founder and director of the World Federation of Hypnotherapists, teaches his students, as part of their course, about regression (present life) and re-regression (past-life). In his own practice, if he finds a patient who is a particularly good subject for hypnosis, he asks them if they would like to try re-regression for interest's sake. If they agree, and with their permission, he records the session. Among the more fascinating of his cases is one of a woman (whom I shall call Judith) who, having regressed to being a young woman in a previous lifetime (we'll call her Alice), went on in a later session to regress to being Alice's mother – who, it is interesting to note, had died at the precise moment her daughter was born.

Another expert in the field of past-life regression, David Reeves, today runs workshops and seminars on the subject in a beautiful old house (a former stately home) in England. The atmosphere of the old building, complete with wood panelling, ancient chapel and, so it is said, resident ghost, is enhanced by the presence of amazing Roman ruins to be found in the grounds.

[II]

WHAT IS HYPNOSIS?

Hypnosis is a perfectly natural condition. It is an altered state of awareness – one that we all reach spontaneously twice a day, once just before waking and once just before going to sleep. It is the link that forms the bridge between the mind and the body.

Yet hypnotherapy is perhaps the most misunderstood of all the complementary therapies. On the one hand, there are those who consider it is only one step away from witchcraft, believing that the hypnotherapist is able to dominate the mind and subjugate the will of an unconscious 'victim'. On the other hand, some people see it as an instant answer to every problem in life. 'Make me stop smoking,' they cry. 'Make me more confident'. The truth is, of course, that no hypnotherapist can make you do anything. His or her skill lies in helping you to achieve your aims for yourself. Even when you see a stage performance of hypnotism and it seems as though the 'unwilling' subjects are being made to act against their will, that is not really the case.

STAGE HYPNOTISM

When performed by someone who is both ethical and properly trained, stage hypnotism is not harmful. It is simply entertainment with willing audience co-operation. Problems can arise, however, when members of the audience who might benefit from clinical hypnotherapy form the wrong impression about hypnosis because of what they see on stage. What these people do not always realize is that those who volunteer to take part in a stage performance are actually the extroverts of the world and would be just as happy 'performing' in some other way. They have been hypnotized because they wished to be and, in psychological terms, perceive the laughter and applause of the audience as a form of love or admiration.

CLINICAL HYPNOSIS

Hypnosis is a state of heightened suggestibility. It is a pleasantly relaxed and drowsy state where all the physiological reflexes (such as knee-jerking) are still present. Although the conscious mind is present and the subject can hear and understand every word spoken, the subject is in a relaxed state that allows the words and suggestions of the therapist to reach the subconscious mind. It is the subconscious mind that has been 'programmed' by incidents and events in the patient's life.

Hypnosis involves complete mental and physical relaxation and, to achieve it, the most important requirement is to have the co-operation of the patient. This is brought about by a combination of the skill and technique of the therapist and the mind and imagination of the patient. Apart from the fact that the correct state will not be reached without that co-operation, it is also a source of comfort to patients to know that they are playing a part in their own cure. Being hypnotized, therefore, is not some purely passive state.

HYPNOTIC TRANCE

I can understand how some people might find the word 'trance' quite frightening. It seems to imply that they will be 'unconscious' or in some way under the influence of the therapist – left without a mind and will of their own. That is not so and it is important to realize that patients always have complete control over their own thoughts and actions at all times. They will not say anything they do not wish to say, nor will they do anything they do not wish to do. All they will feel is pleasantly and comfortably relaxed – but quite capable of hearing and understanding every word spoken to them.

REMOVING BLOCKS

Hypnosis does not, in fact, teach anyone anything new. Everything ever seen, heard or learned is filed away somewhere in the back of the mind. However, hypnosis can help the patient to retrieve these memories, re-discovering skills and aptitudes that already exist. It may turn out that some readjustment and rearrangement of existing skills is required, not to mention the removal of blocks that have been put there – either by the patients themselves or as a result of their experiences with other people.

Hypnosis does not itself cure a single thing. It is the state of heightened sensitivity and increased awareness that allows a cure to take place. During hypnosis, the autonomic nervous system is receptive and, as the subconscious mind is part of that nervous system, it can be reached by the words and suggestions of the therapist without the interference of the patient's conscious mind, with all its accumulated 'programming'. It is therefore possible to get to the root of deep-seated emotional problems and to create in the patient the tools with which to overcome them.

All hypnosis is really self-hypnosis. It is only those patients who co-operate with the therapist and allow themselves to be hypnotized who are, in fact, hypnotized. The fact remains, however, that it is often the very presence of the therapist that gives patients the confidence to allow themselves to be hypnotized in the first place.

INDUCING HYPNOSIS

Forget images of swinging watches – they are no more relevant than the frantic waving of Mesmer's arms. The therapist will simply speak to you, helping you to relax physically and mentally. Sometimes you may be asked to focus your attention on a single point of vision; sometimes you may be asked to close your eyes at the outset.

Hypnotherapy is a skill that must be learnt. It is not, as some people still believe, an almost magical power possessed by just a few. Properly trained hypnotherapists have, like successful doctors, lawyers or musicians, spent a long time studying, practising and perfecting their craft. At the time of writing, there is no one governing body for hypnotherapists, so you should ensure that the one you consult has received proper training. Chapter Two describes some ways of doing this.

CAN EVERYONE BE HYPNOTIZED?

Many people are curious as to who can and who cannot be hypnotized but it is quite simple really. With a few exceptions, detailed below, anyone who wishes to be hypnotized can be – while anyone who does not wish it, cannot. (This applies to the light trance state.)

Children under the age of about five cannot usually concentrate fully enough to co-operate with the therapist in the necessary way. Nor can anyone whose mental faculties are in any way impaired – whether permanently, or temporarily under the influence of alcohol or drugs.

A hypnotherapist would not hypnotize an epilepsy sufferer (even one whose condition is controlled by medication) because there is a slight risk that the altered brain waves could induce a fit. The same applies to those suffering from schizophrenia whose behaviour in the hypnotic state could prove to be negative.

Although children from the age of about five years are usually excellent subjects for hypnosis, it is very rare to find a hypnotherapist willing to use past-life regression with anyone under the age of sixteen. This is because, although it would be possible, it is doubtful whether many very young children would be able to cope emotionally with what they might discover. The exception here is Dr Ian Stevenson who, as has already been seen, is an acknowledged expert in this particular field.

So who makes the ideal subject for hypnosis? The best people are those who possesses the following qualities. They have:

- intelligence,
- a good natural memory,
- a good visual imagination and
- are not afraid to express their feelings.

LEVELS OF HYPNOSIS

There are three main levels of hypnosis: light trance, medium trance and deep trance (also known as the somnambulistic state). To some extent, the level of trance achieved will regulate the outcome of the treatment and for that reason it is worth understanding the differences between them.

Light trance

There are very few people in whom a light trance cannot be induced should they wish it – provided they are willing to co-operate fully with the therapist. This is the state that most people achieve the first time they are hypnotized.

In this state it is not unusual for subjects to think that they have not been hypnotized at all but have simply felt very relaxed for a short time. Indeed, this level of hypnosis rests somewhere between the state of deep relaxation and light meditation. It is ideal for those aspects of therapy that do not need to entail regression: giving up smoking, losing weight, or training the memory, for example. It is not really suitable for those who need or wish to experience regression. They would probably experience some positive results but these would be somewhat superficial and the knowledge gleaned would be of a general rather than a specific nature. However, there is no need to feel that all is lost if at the beginning all you achieve is a light trance. With a little practice and a little help from the therapist, it is quite possible in most cases for the trance level to be deepened sufficiently.

Medium trance

This state can be induced in about three-quarters of the population; the rest, for some unknown reason, cannot achieve it even if they wish to do so. It is, obviously, deeper than the light trance, but not so deep that patients will not be fully aware of what is going on around them. They will actually be able to hear any noises that may occur – a telephone ringing in another room or the traffic in the road outside – but those noises are unlikely to impinge on their consciousness or to interrupt their train of thought. These sounds will merely form part of the background to what is happening. The medium trance is the best one for any treatment requiring regression as it will be possible for the patient to re-live past experiences on a more realistic level, whether seeing and hearing what takes place or being able to describe it as a spectator.

Deep trance

Also known as somnambulistic trance, deep trance can only be attained by 5–10 per cent of the population. It is the form most commonly used in stage hypnotism and the fact that it is beyond the reach of many explains why the stage hypnotist may end up with just ten people to work with out of as many as sixty volunteers. By putting those volunteers through a series of rapid tests on stage, he will soon discover which of them is able to achieve the deep-trance state; it is only these people who will respond quickly and satisfactorily to his suggestions.

I do not believe in using the deep-trance state in any form of therapy as it involves hypnoamnesia, a state in which the patient will be neither aware of what is going on at the time nor able to recall it afterwards. I do not consider this to be ethical in treatment as I believe that everyone should be fully aware of what is happening at each and every stage. Indeed, without such awareness, the patient would be unable to co-operate fully with the therapist and would therefore minimize their chance of a cure. (Throughout this book, when I write in the first person singular, I am really explaining what any ethical hypnotherapist would do. It is just that it is simpler to write from my own experience.)

I have never liked any form of 'mystique' in therapy and always take great pains to explain to my patients precisely what I am going to do at any time, what I expect of them and what they are likely to experience. (For more details on this, see Chapters Three and Nine). Besides, when talking about therapy by hypnosis – whether the problem requires regression or not – deep trance is never necessary.

Even in the deep-trance state, no patient will do or say anything that they would not do or say when fully aware and awake. They will not voluntarily do anything that conflicts with their own personal moral code, nor can they be persuaded to do so. The subconscious mind is at all times fully protective and will not allow the patient to betray themselves by their actions or their words. Even supposing they had committed a murder the previous week, they would not betray that fact under hypnosis if they did not wish to do so!

Those who achieve deep trance cannot usually prevent themselves doing so – it happens spontaneously. They do not consciously hear what is being said to them (although they do 'hear' it on some deep inner level) and often give the appearance of having fallen asleep, although they have not, in fact, done so. This is not really helpful for therapy because the patient will not have sufficient memory of what has occurred to practise for themselves between sessions. Nor is it ideal for regression because patients will not be able to answer the questions put to them by the hypnotherapist as they will not have heard them on a conscious level. Having said that, it is possible to achieve some results by using slightly different techniques but these results may not be as satisfactory for the patient.

edward

Edward was a builder who had been asked to do some repair and maintenance work on a bridge. Unfortunately, he had a fear of heights, so he decided to consult a hypnotherapist for help.

At the first session, the therapist hypnotized Edward, who immediately went into the deep-trance state, appearing to be asleep and unaware of what was being said to him. The hypnotherapist proceeded with the session, using the same words as always for dealing with a fear of heights. At the end of the session, Edward opened his eyes and said that he thought he must have been very tired because he had simply slept through the whole thing. He did not believe that any form of hypnotherapy had taken place. Three days later, Edward telephoned the hypnotherapist to apologize. He had started work on the bridge and was no longer experiencing a fear of heights at all.

LEVELS OF ACTIVITY OF THE MIND

To appreciate fully just what hypnosis really is, it is necessary to understand the way in which the human mind functions. The mind has four different levels of activity. The conscious mind is made up of the Beta and Alpha levels while the unconscious consists of the Theta and Delta levels.

The Beta level

This is the level of consciousness at which we all function during our waking hours – that is for about sixteen hours each day. The primary purpose of this level of activity is to regulate the physical functioning of our bodies, such as breathing, heartbeat, circulation, and so on. Such regulation takes up about three quarters of this level of activity, so that no more than a quarter is available for dealing with our conscious thought processes.

The Alpha level

The Alpha level corresponds to the subconscious mind (as opposed to the 'unconscious' mind – the difference will be explained shortly) and is the level at which we work in hypnotherapy. It involves almost 100 per cent concentration – not available to us in the Beta level. You can see, therefore, that when hypnosis is compared to being 'asleep', nothing could be further from the truth. Neither is it connected to the kind of spontaneous dreams we experience when we are asleep.

Other examples of Alpha-level activity are meditation, daydreaming, and the passage from waking into sleep and from sleeping into wakefulness.

This shows that hypnosis is a perfectly natural state of mind and that the hypnotized subjects may be relaxed physically but are also fully aware of what is happening and being said around them.

The Theta level

This level corresponds to that part of the unconscious mind (as opposed to the 'subconscious' mind), which functions when we are in a light sleep. In fact, by far the greater part of all sleep takes place on this level. The word 'conscious' means that we are awake and aware while 'unconscious' implies that we are unawake and unaware.

The Delta level

This is the deep-sleep level that, perhaps surprisingly, usually occupies no more than about thirty minutes each night. During that time, the unconscious mind is obtaining the maximum amount of rest. The length of time one is asleep before reaching this level varies considerably from person to person.

At the Delta level, no hypnotic suggestion can be heard – so you will see that it is very different to the case of Edward who may have appeared to be asleep but who was, in fact, in the deep-trance state.

Hypnosis and the Alpha state

To be hypnotized is to put aside the conscious mind and deal directly with the subconscious. When we are functioning at full consciousness (the Beta state), both conscious and subconscious minds will be working. There are three differences between that state and the state of hypnosis:

1 Powers of concentration are much sharper when one is hypnotized. This is because, as has already been explained, almost 100 per cent of the conscious mind will be involved, as opposed to 25 per cent when not hypnotized.
2 The body is totally relaxed and often feels heavy and warm. In addition, some people experience a slight tingling sensation (not unlike pins and needles) but this is very gentle and not at all unpleasant.
3 Although subjects are capable of moving and changing position at any time, they often feel that they do not want to do this. It is as though their mind is so sharp and so aware that the body ceases to matter. It is not unusual for people to find that the aches and pains of the day disappear when they are in a state of hypnosis.

DAYDREAMING

There is little difference between hypnosis and daydreaming – except that the former is usually deliberately brought about and often guided by a therapist whereas the latter occurs spontaneously in most cases.

When we daydream we tend to lose all sense of place and time and our thoughts are concentrated on the subject of the daydream. We are, in fact, in the Alpha state, having entered it entirely naturally. So all those people who believe that they 'couldn't be hypnotized' have actually entered the same 'trance state' as those who have deliberately sought to do so.

SELF-KNOWLEDGE

Hypnosis in general – and both present and past-life regression in particular – can be great aids to an individual's self-knowledge and this can only be a good thing. They can help us to understand why we behave as we do, what caused us to do so and the effect that other people and external events have had on our lives. They can also help us to bring to the forefront of the mind those things that we have forgotten and that may be significant when considering the type of person we are today and how we are to deal with any problems we may have.

There has been much speculation in recent years about false-memory syndrome, particularly in cases where adults appear to 'remember' incidences of abuse in their childhood and then go on to accuse the alleged perpetrators.

When a regression session (past- or present-life) is conducted by a properly qualified and ethical hypnotherapist, there can be no danger of accusations of false-memory syndrome. It is never the task of the therapist to suggest anything that might have happened in the subject's past. Questions asked would be such as, 'What happened next?', 'Where did you go?', and so on, so that any facts given during the course of answers would be entirely unprompted.

PRESENT-LIFE REGRESSION

When people are confronted with an event or a situation that is extremely traumatic, their instinctive reaction is often to block it from the memory. Sometimes this is done deliberately and the person concerned refuses to think about it at all. At other times the subconscious mind — which is ever-protective — ensures that they are no longer troubled by the memories.

In many cases treatment is improved — and certainly accelerated — when such memories are brought to the forefront of the mind. If the person has done a very good job of blocking them from the conscious mind, it is only possible to recall them with the aid of hypnotic regression.

Although the discovery of the root cause of a particular problem does not in itself provide a cure, it is certainly a highly significant stepping-stone on the road to recovery, laying the foundation for any treatment that is to follow. It can also prove significant for those who are on a journey of spiritual exploration and discovery. A series of regressions can be highly beneficial as it can bring to light the pattern so far and, therefore, allows the subject to make decisions about future progress.

sylvia

Sylvia had been frightened of birds for as long as she could remember. In the beginning, the problem had not been too bad — although she would never approach a bird (even a caged one) and did not even care to see pictures of them. But, as time progressed, and in the manner of all phobias, her condition worsened. By the time she sought the help of a hypnotherapist she was so afraid of coming across groups of sparrows or pigeons in her path that she almost became a prisoner in her own home.

With Sylvia's consent, I decided to regress her to an earlier stage in her present life. On the second occasion, Sylvia talked of a time when she was two years old and was sitting in a pushchair being taken for a walk to the park by her mother.

At the park, her mother met another young woman and they stopped to talk, neither of them looking at Sylvia in her pushchair. Suddenly a bird flew past the little girl, coming so close that she felt its wings brush her face. She screamed but, by the time her mother looked to see what was happening, the bird had flown away.

Talking of this event while under hypnosis, Sylvia explained that it was not just the nearness of the bird that had frightened her but the fact that she was at the time firmly strapped into her pushchair and was unable to move away. Over the years, this event had built up in her mind to create the phobia that was now seriously troubling her.

The knowledge of this incident was not sufficient in itself to bring about a cure but it did prove to Sylvia that there was a reason for her phobia and that she was not 'stupid' or 'different' because she suffered from it. Starting from this point of knowledge, it was only necessary for Sylvia to have three more sessions with me for her fears to be dispelled for ever.

FEARS AND ANXIETIES ABOUT HYPNOSIS

Before going any further, perhaps it would be as well to dispel some of the more common myths and fears concerning the subject of hypnosis and to explain my own particular way of working.

As I have said, if a patient does not wish to be hypnotized, then all the skill and expertise in the world will not induce that state in them. Of course, by the time patients come to see me, they have usually made up their mind that hypnosis will be beneficial for them and so I do not encounter an unwillingness to be hypnotized very often. I always spend the greater part of the first session explaining just what is going to happen and how they are going to feel; as a result I hope that, by the time we begin the hypnosis itself, the patient will have had all their questions answered and their fears allayed and will have begun to feel confidence in me and in what I am about to do.

It is not unusual for someone to wonder whether undergoing hypnosis is likely to induce any unpleasant or harmful side-effects. In all the years I have been practising, and among all the hypnotherapists whom I know or of whom I have read, I have never heard of patients suffering side-effects – except positive ones – of any kind. The first stage of hypnosis involves learning to relax – something that we can all benefit from – so any side-effects experienced are likely to be highly therapeutic. You may find that you are sleeping better than before (and can throw away any sleeping pills you may have been taking), that you have got rid of that nagging headache, and that the muscles in your neck and shoulders are suddenly starting to feel warm and relaxed.

You can be confident that no harm will ever come to you through hypnosis. Remember that you are always the one who is in control and, if there is anything that makes you feel at all anxious, all you have to do is open your eyes and the session will be over. This will do you no harm at all – although, of course, to be brought gently back to the present by the voice of the therapist is a more satisfactory way of concluding the proceedings.

When bringing patients out of the hypnotized state I usually count to three. This allows them time to come back gradually to a state of full awareness without any sense of shock. However, it would be just as effective if I were to snap my fingers or even simply to tell them to 'wake up'.

Some people also fear that after the session they will be left in a semi-hypnotized state. Or even, as one of my own patients once asked me, 'What will happen if you hypnotize me and then drop dead before you wake me up?' Much as I hope this will never occur, all that would occur is that patients would either open their eyes and come out of the hypnotic state completely, or that they might doze for some ten or fifteen minutes before waking as if from a nap in an armchair.

There are some patients who make wonderful subjects for hypnotic therapy but who are unable to relax sufficiently for regression. This is normally because they have some fear, conscious or otherwise, about what they will unearth during the course of the treatment. Once again, by the time I have talked to them, explained how regression works and just what they will experience, I would hope that they would feel confident enough in me and in themselves to allow it to take place. As I shall explain more fully in the next chapter, it is quite possible to ensure that they do not suffer in any way at all, whether mentally, physically or emotionally.

Bear in mind, however, that hypnosis is not a party game to be practised by amateurs for the amusement of themselves or of others. It is not difficult to learn a simple technique of inducing a hypnotic state in another person – it is knowing how to deal with that person once they have been hypnotized that is important and not something to be indulged in for fun. While this would not do any permanent harm to the person being hypnotized, it is not right to treat anyone's problems as subject matter for frivolous experiment.

If hypnosis, in any form, is to be taken seriously, then it is even more important that hypnotic regression is treated with due respect. The person who is being regressed may come face to face with something that was either traumatic at the time or that may have seemed trivial but has turned out to have had a long-lasting subconscious effect, so the whole subject needs careful and skilful handling. At the end of this book you will find the address of an organization that can supply you with the name of an ethical professional hypnotherapist in your area, should you require one.

It is possible to buy cassette tapes that are supposed to enable you to experiment with regression yourself. I cannot urge you strongly enough to resist the temptation of trying to work with such tapes. They claim to help you begin a regression by yourself and then leave you to see where it takes you. All might go well and you might simply re-live and re-experience a happy time in your present or past-life. The danger arises if you happen to arrive at what was for you a distressing time and there is no one there to help you deal with it. There is, however, no harm at all in using professional hypnotic cassettes that are designed to assist you in overcoming a specific problem where regression is not needed – such as dealing with smoking addiction, aiding your studying, treating pre-menstrual tension, and so on. On these cassettes you will hear the voice of the hypnotherapist who will help you to achieve the desired state, then give you the same suggestions that he or she would have given if you had been in the consulting room; finally the hypnotherapist will wake you up again.

When a patient comes to me for regression, I do in fact record the session on cassette, giving the tape to the patient at the end of the consultation. But these tapes will have blank passages on them, for I never, never record the actual technique. This is not because it is so special or secret that I do not want to divulge it – indeed patients will remember it quite well for themselves – but because I do not want them to listen to that cassette at some time in the future and begin to regress themselves when I am not there to take charge of the situation. So the recording will not even begin until patients have reached that point in their memory that they wish to explore and, should it be necessary to move them forwards or backwards in time within that regression, I simply place my hand over the microphone so that, once again, the technique is not recorded.

THE BENEFIT OF SELF-KNOWLEDGE

As I pointed out earlier, regression itself does not provide the cure to any particular problem. It is merely a first step – but a very significant one and one without which the hypnotherapist's task would certainly be made far more difficult.

There are some problems (such as stopping smoking, improving memory, preventing nail-biting, and so on) that can be dealt with satisfactorily without the need for regression. But, apart from the fact that there are some patients who, however straightforward their problem may seem, insist upon knowing what caused it in the first place, self-understanding is the key to the successful resolution of any emotional problem.

This is particularly relevant when dealing with people who suffer from phobias. The dictionary defines phobia as an 'illogical fear' and sufferers are often only too well aware that their phobia is, indeed, illogical. This fact does nothing to bolster their confidence in themselves; without that feeling of self-confidence they will find it extremely difficult to work towards overcoming their fear. If, through regression, patients find the reason for the onset of the phobia – that first, frightening occasion – although that knowledge may not be sufficient in itself to put an end to the problem, it certainly stops the sufferer feeling that they are simply being 'weak' and 'foolish' or (as one of my patients put it) that 'I am going out of my mind'. This, in turn, puts them in the right frame of mind to be helped to overcome the problem once and for all.

So, while regression cannot be claimed to be the be-all and end-all of therapeutic treatment, it is certainly an important stage. To miss out would mean the treatment itself would take far longer, if indeed it were to succeed at all.

[III]

WHAT TO EXPECT

There are various reasons why people decide to experience past-life regression. Some people have a present-day problem that they feel has its root cause at some time in a past life. Others are on a path of spiritual self-awareness and realize that the more knowledge they have of the various lives they have lived, the more they will be able to work towards their personal evolvement. And there are those who attend sessions for no more reason than curiosity – they want to know whether they did live past lives and, if so, what those lives were like.

Whatever their initial reason for seeking past-life regression, each of those people can benefit from the experience.

DEALING WITH A PRESENT-DAY PROBLEM

The person with a current problem for which they can see no reason can be helped to find the cause – and therefore the cure. Quite often this problem is a phobia of some sort. As explained previously, a phobia is defined in the dictionary as an 'illogical fear', but this definition does little to help the self-esteem of sufferers. Not only do they have their fear to contend with but the fact that it is termed 'illogical' makes them feel foolish and inferior.

We have already seen how this sense of foolishness can be relieved in some cases by regression to an earlier time in the patient's present life – as in the case of the woman who was frightened of birds. But sometimes, however hard one searches, there appears to be no root cause at any time in the patient's current existence. Indeed, there are cases where it is possible to take the person back to the moment of birth only to discover that the fear already exists – they have 'brought it with them'. In such cases, past-life regression would be the next step in their treatment.

spiritual evolvement

To someone who is seeking enlightenment on their personal spiritual growth, past lives play an important role. If it is a fact that our spirit travels through life after life as it evolves, then the more that is known about each of those lives, the more clearly that journey towards evolvement can be understood. Reasons can be seen for the mistakes we all make in each of our lives and the lessons learned from those mistakes can be put in context and understood so that we never have to make them again.

In addition, because it is often possible to recognize the presence of the same people in life after life (although they may appear in different guises, playing different roles), it helps to understand the people around us now, why some are so important to us and in what way this is so.

curiosity

Those people who want to delve into their past lives purely out of curiosity may also gain great benefit. Although these lives do not present themselves in any sort of chronological order, it is possible after experiencing three or four to place them in order of time and to examine them to see whether there is a recurring pattern.

george

Some years ago, a businessman called George was curious to find out whether he had, in fact, lived in the past. He said that he was not seeking any deep or meaningful answers to questions but simply wanted to satisfy his inquisitiveness. Over a period of time, George experienced six different past lives, and asked his secretary to transcribe the cassettes he received after each one. Placing them in chronological order, the theme that repeated itself became quite clear to see. In each one of those lives, from 1642 onwards, George had been given the opportunity to be a guide, teacher or counsellor to others – and in each one of those lives he had rejected the opportunity and pursued his own interests, thinking little of those other people.

Even to George – who had never considered himself to be a particularly spiritual person – it seemed obvious that this was something he was 'meant' to do. In fact, at an earlier stage in his present-day life, he had trained to be a Samaritan but had given it up to concentrate solely on his business interests.

At the end of his last session he said that, although he would always be a businessman first and foremost, he was also going to try to think of ways in which he could be of help to others. So you can see that, whatever the reason for any individual to seek past-life regression – and even when there seems to be no particular reason at all – a great deal may be achieved as a result.

The right hypnotherapist for the right person

Hypnosis is very much a one-to-one process, requiring co-operation between therapist and subject. Because of this, it is very important that you feel comfortable with the therapist you are working with. However well qualified he or she may be, if this link between you both does not exist, the results will be

far less effective. The following are a few points to bear in mind once you have
found a hypnotherapist.

- Never be afraid to ask a hypnotherapist about his or her training,
  qualifications and insurance.
- Any hypnotherapist should be willing to spend ten to fifteen minutes talking
  to you – without charge – to answer your questions in order to put your mind
  at rest before you decide to go ahead with the treatment.
- Beware of therapists who try to convince you that they have 'special powers'
  or who are unwilling to explain each stage of the process to you.
- Avoid someone who tries to charge you for a complete course of treatment
  at the outset. It is impossible to know how many sessions particular patients
  are going to need until you have worked with them.
- Listen to other people. There is no better recommendation than the word of
  someone whose opinion you respect.
- Trust your intuition. If you do not feel at ease with a particular therapist, he
  or she is not the one for you.

THE BENEFITS OF PAST-LIFE REGRESSION

Whatever the personal spiritual or religious beliefs of any individual, no one can
deny that knowing and understanding more about oneself can only be beneficial.
Past-life regression is another tool we can use to help in gleaning this extra
knowledge. The fact that this knowledge comes from within ourselves – as
opposed to being told to us by another person – can only add to its credibility
and validity.

The spiritual path

Ideas about our spiritual progress can vary from person to person but what
follows is the generally held belief of most of those who have been involved in
any way in past-life regression, whether as practitioner or subject. It would
appear that, although each human body eventually dies and is disposed of in
whatever way is thought appropriate, the spirit continues from one body to
another – and has done so for many generations. It is that spirit that never
forgets and that we touch when experiencing past-life regression.

Making choices

The most widely held belief is that, when the time comes for the spirit to enter a 'new' human being, it actually chooses the life it is to lead – who are to be its parents, where it is to be born and so on. It also chooses the lessons it is to be faced with in the coming lifetime and what it hopes to learn from those lessons.

All human beings have a mind and a will of their own. There is no such thing as absolute predestination (which would make us little more than pawns on life's chessboard, able to move only where we are placed) so it is the human being who makes the decisions during his or her lifetime, doing things in the right or wrong way when faced with choices created by those lessons. As a result of the human being's behaviour, those lessons are either profited from or they are not.

Lessons repeated

If, because of the actions of the human being, the wrong choices are made during any particular lifetime, then the spirit has to face the same ones again in its subsequent life. It is rather like a child who has not progressed satisfactorily and is kept back to repeat a school year.

Suppose, for example, one spirit had chosen the lesson of 'forgiveness' for a particular lifetime. The human being might find him or herself faced with the opportunity to forgive someone who has wronged him. If that forgiveness is forthcoming, the spirit can progress to the next lesson; if it is not, the next body the spirit inhabits will be faced with the same need to learn how to forgive.

Reducing the fear of death

Once you believe in the concept of reincarnation, how can death hold the terrors it may once have done? That is not to say that anyone actively looks forward to dying but it is a great comfort to know that there is a 'somewhere else' – even if we are not really sure what that 'somewhere else' is like.

Similarly, if there is another place to go to, it follows that this place exists for your loved ones too. So, when someone close to you dies, there is no need to feel that you will never be with them again. No one can explain exactly how you will meet or what the place will be like but, among those who accept the concept of reincarnation, there is absolutely no doubt that you will do so.

Near-death experiences

There are few people who have not heard of someone who has had a near-death experience. Perhaps they have been very close to death while in hospital – or perhaps they have even technically 'died' for a moment or two. It is interesting to note how such people, when they recover, immediately seem to lose all sense of fear about their future death, whenever it may be.

The details revealed in the descriptions of their experiences may vary a little but this is far outweighed by the similarities. None of them will have found the process frightening or painful – indeed some will tell you that they were aware of actively trying to get to the wonderful place they knew lay ahead of them but were prevented from doing so by some greater force.

The other comforting fact mentioned by those who have had a near-death experience is that we do not go to the special place alone. Almost without exception they will tell of the person who was there to greet them and accompany them on their journey.

PAST-LIFE REGRESSION USING NON-HYPNOTIC METHODS

Hypnosis is not the only method of inducing past-life regression. In fact there are several others. But for the reasons given here, it is often felt that hypnosis is more effective, safer and more convincing than any other technique.

spontaneous regression

Many people speak of brief experiences of déjà vu, but spontaneous regression of a deep nature is comparatively rare. Even incidences of déjà vu can be suspect. Many of us have experienced that feeling of 'I've been here before' when visiting a place for what we know to be the first time. But, with the growth of cinema and television, we have all seen places that we later visit. It may be that we have not registered the fact that we have seen such a place – a film could be set in a particular location and we are so involved with the story that the background scenery enters only the subconscious mind. When we eventually visit that place in reality, the subconscious memory is triggered and we convince ourselves that we knew intuitively what it would look like.

That is not to say that genuine déjà vu does not exist – there are incidences when it has been proved to do so – but probably not nearly as often as is claimed.

meditative regression

Perhaps the only people who may experience in-depth periods of spontaneous regression are those who are in the habit of practising deep meditation on a regular basis. The state of deep meditation is similar to that of hypnosis and many of those who have an interest in the practice of meditation are often on a journey of spiritual discovery so it may be possible for them to pass through those protective barriers normally put in place by the subconscious mind.

Dreams

It is possible to have what appear to be instances of past-life regression while dreaming. There is, however, no way of ascertaining whether such instances are genuine recall, figments of the imagination – or a combination of the two. So many of our dreams are a mixture of fact and fantasy that it would appear difficult to place any reliance on what appear to be examples of past-life regression while in that state.

The christos technique

This is a method of inducing past-life regression that has the reputation of being both safe and effective. It involves the assistance of a helper who first massages the feet of the subject, and then the head, and finally guides him or her through a meditation exercise intended to lead to the regression itself. It is thought that this method originated in the United States, from where it travelled to Australia – but there are conflicting reports as to its true origins. The current acknowledged expert is G M Glaskin who has written extensively on the subject.

There are two aspects about the Christos Technique that also appear in the hypnotic technique and that most people would consider essential in the interests of safety and authenticity.

- Another person is present at all times to assist subjects in entering the regressed state and also to help them avoid any difficulty or distress.
- The 'evidence' comes from subjects themselves and is not given to them by someone else.

psychic or astrological evidence

Good psychics and good astrologers exist and may even be able to tell you psychically who you were in a past life, or draw up a chart to do so, but you have no way of knowing whether what they say to you is actually true because such methods are open to abuse by the unscrupulous. They cannot prove that they are right and you cannot prove that they are wrong. Such methods, even when genuine, cannot compare with the facts and emotions brought to the fore when you experience a personal regression for yourself.

The value of using hypnosis

There are many reasons for thinking that hypnosis is the best method of inducing past-life regression:

- Another person will be with you constantly and will be able to guide you into the appropriate altered state of mind.
- Any evidence comes from yourself and is not simply told to you by someone else.
- Hypnosis involves deep relaxation and a release of tension that can only be beneficial to the subject.
- Use of the detachment technique (more details later) ensures that, however traumatic the past life may have been, the subject does not experience any discomfort or distress.

OTHER THEORIES

Over the years, other theories have been put forward for what appears to be past-life regression. There are thoughts about memory – personally inherited or ancestral – as well as discussions on the theory of thought transference. The concept of time and how we perceive it is thought by some to affect our understanding of what we believe to be our past lives. Others put the whole thing down to indoctrination or simple imaginings.

Ancestral memory

The Swiss psychologist Carl Gustav Jung, among others, put forward the theory that when it appears that an individual is recalling a past life, what that person is actually doing is tuning in to some vast ancestral 'memory bank' from which he or she is able to draw facts and details. Jung pointed out that this did not mean that past lives did not exist – merely that it might be extremely difficult, if not impossible, to differentiate between remembered facts from a time when an individual spirit had lived before and those facts that were gleaned from some perpetual and world-wide book of knowledge.

Personally inherited memory

There are those who claim that what appear to be examples of reincarnation are really examples of memory that was inherited along with the genes that dictate our physical characteristics, and so on. To back up their argument, they ask us to look at animals who, even if they lose their mother at birth, know instinctively how to do those things that all others of their species can do. Why, they ask, does a cat living with an indulgent owner who provides good food at regular intervals still maintain the instinct to hunt for mice, shrews and birds? And how does that same cat know how to wash itself in precisely the same way as every other cat?

Proponents of this theory suggest that, if such knowledge is inherited from the parent cat, it is possible that any memories we may appear to have of past lives have been inherited too. While not being able to disprove this statement, it is widely felt that there is a great deal of difference between our basic behaviour and the remembrance of events and people from the past. Left to its own devices, a baby will pull itself up to a sitting and then a standing position before learning to walk – just as the cat washes or hunts in a particular way. This does not indicate that everything that baby grows up to remember has been inherited too.

cryptomnesia

Cryptomnesia means the recall of something that people have actually seen or heard at an earlier stage in their current life but they have either forgotten the fact or were not consciously aware of it at the time. In some cases, this could possibly be true, but there are also documented instances of times when knowledge was displayed by a child who was too young to have travelled anywhere alone and who was as yet unable to read or write.

Thought transference

Some people believe that the 'memories' recounted by someone during a session of past-life regression are, in fact, details they have picked up by psychically receiving transferred thoughts from the person conducting the regression session. This means that, no matter how careful the therapist is to avoid leading or guiding the subject by their questions, that subject is still able to give the answers the therapist expects to hear. Speaking for myself, I can only say that on many of the occasions that I have been conducting a regression session, the answers given by subjects have been a complete surprise to me and not what I was expecting at all. Not only that but, on occasion, details have been given of facts of which I had no knowledge whatsoever so I do not feel there would have been any way in which I could have 'psychically transferred' them to the person being regressed.

The meaning of time

The concept of time was invented by human beings in order that there might be a framework upon which to build the progress of their lives. It is believed by some that, if time itself does not really exist, then it is not possible for us to have past – or future – lives. If one imagines that somewhere to one side of us Henry VIII is reigning while, far away on the other side, it is the year 3000, the argument is that those who appear to be experiencing past lives are really only seeing momentarily through the mist that divides those events.

Imagination

It is not suggested that many people would deliberately fabricate what appears to be a past life. For most people – with the exception of those who will do anything to be the centre of attention – that would be a pretty pointless exercise. But it is thought by some that all past-life regressions are actually examples of the over-active imagination of the participants.

PAST LIFE RATHER THAN PRESENT LIFE

When a hypnotherapist is trying to help patients overcome a particular problem, it is very common to use what is known as hypnoanalysis. This involves taking patients back to an earlier time in their present life to see if the cause of the current problem can be discovered. Sometimes, however, this is not enough. If, despite all efforts, nothing can be found in the current life of patients that could account for the problem from which they are suffering, it is usually effective to look to their former lives. However the original cause is discovered, the knowledge of it does not in itself constitute a cure. It is, however, a very significant first step and can often make subsequent treatment shorter and more dramatically successful.

Margaret

Margaret had been afraid of water for as long as anyone could remember. It wasn't just that she was too nervous to learn to swim, whether in a pool or in the sea – after all, she could have lived her life quite happily without becoming a swimmer. But it had reached the stage where she didn't even like to have a bath unless there were no more than a couple of inches of water around her. It was at this point that she came to me for help. There did not seem to be any basis for Margaret's fear in her current lifetime so it was decided to see whether a trigger could be found in the past.

In her first regression session, Margaret went back to a life when she was a small girl living with her family in East Anglia. One day, after weeks of heavy rain, the floods came and the whole family had to flee from their home, leaving most of their possessions behind them. Margaret could clearly recall being carried high on her father's shoulders as he ran for safety.

The interesting thing about this regression was that, when Margaret was taken to a later stage in that same life, although she could remember the incident, she had not at that time developed any fear of water. The present-day Margaret, when brought out of the regression, found this very reassuring as it proved that there had been a time – however long ago – when the sight, sound and feel of water had not induced in her any sense of panic at all.

The second time she was regressed, Margaret went back to a life when she was a young man called Tom, who was apprenticed to a wheelwright in a nearby village. One summer evening, Tom was walking home by the river after the day's work. He was tired but happy having just been given his money for the month. Suddenly Tom was set upon by two youths who beat him about the head and body with heavy sticks and, when he lay injured on the ground, kicked him viciously before robbing him of his earnings. Tom struggled to his feet and tried to get his money back but the two louts hit him again before picking him up and throwing him into the river. Injured, unable to swim and with no one there to hear his cries for help, Tom drowned.

In the discussion that followed, Margaret could see how her experience as Tom could have caused her present dread of water. Not only had she drowned but, prior to that, she had been through a time of pain and fear during the attack she had suffered. In addition, having been thrown into the river, she had been dragged under the surface of the water by the current, only to rise again, fighting for breath, until finally she was unable to survive.

In her subconscious mind, a strong link had been forged between water, fear and pain – a link that she had brought with her into her current lifetime. Knowing the cause of her water phobia and understanding that it was not foolishness on her part but a condition with a very logical cause, Margaret and I were able to go on together to help her overcome those fears once and for all.

[IV]

QUESTIONS AND ANSWERS

Many people are somewhat apprehensive about undergoing a session of past-life regression for the first time. This is quite understandable – any new experience can be a little daunting and, in this case, the technique and possibly even the therapist may be unknown to them. The following section, written in question-and-answer form, covers the points most frequently raised by a prospective subject.

CAN ANYONE BE REGRESSED TO A PAST LIFE?

Anyone who is suitable for hypnosis and who wishes it can be regressed to a past life. Fear of what will happen, whether conscious or subconscious, can prevent a regression session being successful but all such fears should have been set aside by discussion with the hypnotherapist before the regression was actually attempted.

DO ALL HYPNOTHERAPISTS PRACTISE PAST-LIFE REGRESSION?

No. The number of hypnotherapists practising past-life regression is increasing as interest in the topic grows among the public. But some hypnotherapists have no real desire to work in this field and, for others, it may actually be against their religious beliefs even to contemplate doing so.

HOW WILL I BE HYPNOTIZED?

It is most likely that a vocal induction will be used. This means that you will be asked to close your eyes and the hypnotherapist will talk to you, encouraging you to relax your muscles and regulate your breathing. This technique is not unlike some forms of yoga. The therapist will then count you down into the trance state.

HOW WILL I FEEL?

You will feel very relaxed and very comfortable – very much as you do when you are tucked up in your bed at night, just prior to dropping off to sleep. It is important to remember, however, that your mind will be in complete control at all times. You will hear and understand every word spoken to you. You will not 'lose consciousness' nor 'fall asleep'.

CAN I EAT OR DRINK BEFORE A SESSION?

Once again, comfort is the important thing here. It is sensible not to eat an enormous meal just before the session – but, equally, it would be foolish to starve yourself so that all you could think of is how hungry you are. It is probably advisable not to have alcohol just before the session as that, combined with the relaxation technique, might send you to sleep. This would not only waste everyone's time but also your money too.

DO I HAVE TO WEAR ANYTHING SPECIAL?

It is essential that you are comfortable, so it is best not to wear anything that is stiff or tight. Avoid high collars, tight waistbands or uncomfortable shoes (in fact, many people prefer to remove their shoes, and this is quite acceptable). You are going to have your eyes closed for quite a while – probably at least twenty minutes – so, if you normally wear contact lenses, you might feel more comfortable if you remove them.

WHAT IF I AM TAKING PRESCRIBED MEDICATION?

Bearing in mind that epileptics and schizophrenics should not be hypnotized, there is no medication that can adversely affect the hypnotic session. Similarly, hypnosis cannot cause you harm, no matter what condition you might be suffering from and what medication you are taking.

DO I NEED TO HAVE A GOOD VISUAL IMAGINATION?

The ability to visualize is of great benefit, not only for a session of past-life regression but also for hypnotherapy in general. With the exception of those who were born blind, everyone has the ability to 'see pictures in their head'. Because of western education and the pressures of everyday life, many of us lose this ability as we grow older. If you feel that this may have happened to you, try following the series of exercises below to improve your ability to visualize.

visualization exercise

1 Select a simple object – such as a cup, vase, or lamp. Look at it for several minutes, studying its shape, colour, size and so on. Now close your eyes and try to see it in your mind in as much detail as possible. If you find this difficult, simply open your eyes and start again.

2 Once you can do the above, try doing the same thing with a group of three or four objects.

3 Now think of a place you knew well in your recent or distant past. Visualize it in as much detail as possible, trying to include the atmosphere as well as the physical sights. When you have achieved this, you will know that there is nothing wrong with your visual imagination.

Don't expect to improve your ability to visualize in a single session. Think of your imagination as a muscle. If you wish to improve the strength of any of the muscles in your body, you would work on that area repeatedly until you had achieved the desired effect. Similarly, repeating the above exercise will serve to improve the 'muscles' of your visual imagination.

HOW WILL THE HYPNOTHERAPIST REGRESS ME?

He or she will induce a normal state of hypnosis and then go on to a particular spoken method of taking you back to a time when you lived before. (It is not appropriate to print the actual words of a regression here as someone who does not have sufficient background knowledge of the technique might be tempted to use them.)

WHAT DO I HAVE TO DO DURING THE REGRESSION?

All that is required of you is that you are willing to co-operate with the hypnotherapist while he or she takes you gently through the relaxation exercise into the hypnotic state. Perhaps the most important thing you can do is keep an open mind. Try not to start with pre-conceived ideas. Just let the process take its course and see what happens – as though you were reading a good book or watching an interesting film and waiting to see what comes next. You will not be asked to speak during the induction stage – although you would certainly be capable of doing so. It is also helpful if you try not to question what is happening during the session itself. Of course questioning is healthy and to be desired – but try to keep this until the discussion afterwards. The link between your present and past life is fragile, so it is not difficult to break if you allow too much logical thought to get in the way. So try to answer the questions spontaneously, saying the first thing that comes into your head, even if that thought seems unlikely.

HOW LONG WILL THE SESSION LAST?

The entire session will probably last about an hour – but, of that time, you will only be actively regressed for about twenty minutes or so. This is because the brain tends to lose concentration after this period of time and so you would be less able to sustain the regression.

The length of the consultation allows for a preliminary talk, during which the hypnotherapist will explain everything to you and, hopefully, allay any fears or apprehensions you might have, and also ensures there is time for a discussion afterwards, when you will have the opportunity to talk about your experience and ask any questions that might occur to you.

HOW MANY SESSIONS OF PAST-LIFE REGRESSION WILL I NEED?

There is no definite answer to this question as much will depend upon your reasons for wanting to be regressed in the first place. If your regression is part of ongoing therapy, it is likely that one or two sessions will suffice. If you are trying to find out more about your personal evolvement, or you have come out of simple curiosity, you might wish to have several more sessions in order to increase your knowledge.

HOW FREQUENT SHOULD THESE SESSIONS BE?

Again, the answer depends upon the reason you are being regressed in the first place. If you are being helped to overcome some current problem, there may be no more than two weeks before sessions. In the other cases it is preferable to leave at least six weeks between sessions. This is because you will often find that further information about a previous life comes into your head spontaneously over the few weeks following the regression and it might prove too confusing to have too many sessions close together.

HOW WILL I KNOW WHETHER I HAVE EXPERIENCED A REAL PAST-LIFE REGRESSION OR WHETHER IT IS ALL A PRODUCT OF MY IMAGINATION?

This is quite a difficult question to answer. Some people are absolutely convinced that what they have experienced during a regression session really was a glimpse of a previous life. Other people may not be quite so sure. But, as mentioned before, perhaps it really does not matter. If the aim of the regression was to help the patient overcome a present-day problem and it does so, then the aim has been achieved whether the regression was genuine or not. If patients are seeking to satisfy curiosity or to develop a greater general awareness of a spiritual direction, then, even if the regression results from their imaginings, it has validity in that there must be some reason why their mind has chosen to come up with one set of facts, dates, details and personalities rather than another. It should be repeated here, however, that there have been innumerable instances of details being revealed during past-life regression that have later been verified, so most therapists working in this field are totally convinced that reincarnation exists and that it is possible for us to tap into our own past lives – even if not every single case is a true example of this.

HOW WILL FACTS BE BROUGHT TO LIGHT?

In most cases, once you have been regressed, the therapist will ask you questions that you will answer. This may be recorded on cassette so that you can take it away and use it as you wish afterwards. (However, many therapists do not record the technique. This is not because it is secret – indeed you will remember the session yourself quite well – but they feel it would not be advisable for you to listen to the technique on tape and start a process that you might not be able to control).

HOW DO I FIND A REPUTABLE HYPNOTHERAPIST?

At the time of writing there is no single governing body for hypnotherapy. There are many organizations and colleges, each of which has its own register. At the end of this book you will find an address to contact that should provide you with the names and addresses of therapists in your area who practise past-life regression.

REINCARNATION

There are those who say that, because reincarnation cannot yet be proved to the satisfaction of the scientific fraternity, it does not exist. But many of those who have experienced past-life regression for themselves believe there is no doubt at all that it exists and that they have been able to learn about some of their own previous incarnations. Some of the questions most commonly asked about reincarnation include:

what happens between incarnations?

It is not possible to prove beyond doubt exactly how long the spirit spends elsewhere before choosing to enter the body of another person. However, there is a generally-held opinion that there is an interval of approximately seventy years between lives. The exception to this seems to be when a person dies suddenly or at a very young age. In such cases the spirit seems to return after a much shorter interval – almost as though it had unfinished business to complete (see below). There are different theories about what happens between incarnations. Some think of it as a period of rest, healing and meditation for the spirit. Others see it is a time of learning for the spirit – but that this learning occurs in some higher place than any we know.

Many people believe this is a time when the spirit is watching over the next two generations – particularly their own offspring, if they had any. If you think about family life, this is quite understandable. We care very much for our children and grandchildren but, by the time the next generation comes along, our attitude towards them is likely to be more detached. It makes sense, therefore, that when we die we are anxious to ensure that our children and grandchildren are safe and well but we leave the observation of the well-being of later generations to their parents or grandparents.

what about those who die before reaching the normal age for the period?

If someone's life comes to an end, whether through ill health, accident or violence, before what would be deemed normal for the age they are living in, those people seem to be reincarnated some time before the seventy years already mentioned. It could be that they need to complete anything unfinished from the previous life or that, having died young, they do not have two further generations to care about from the spirit world. The exception to this appears to be following the death of a baby – whether at the moment of birth or within the first twelve months or so. These spirits often do not seem to be reincarnated at all, leading to the thought that they were in fact so evolved that they did not need to come back to earth to learn any further lessons. They had actually completed their earthly education and perhaps only needed to touch the lives of those around them for a brief moment in order to help those other people learn something too.

why are there differing theories about reincarnation?

No one can prove what actually happens. All we can do is speak from our own experience and belief, whether as the person undergoing regression, the therapist involved in helping this to take place or a spiritualist medium whose purpose in life is to bring comfort to others by proving the survival of the spirit. Think of an incident that is observed by several different people. When each person gives their account of what happened, you are likely to find several discrepancies. This does not mean that anyone is lying – merely that the individuals see the incident from their own viewpoint, in the light of their previous experiences and their own individuality. Why should the same not be true of the experience and understanding of reincarnation?

As there are more people on earth now than there were hundreds of years ago, how can they all have past lives?

There is no reason to think that new spirits cannot be born or created and, indeed, this is probably happening all the time. A new spirit who is in an earthly body for the first time would not have a past life to explore – but you would also find that he or she had no interest in doing so. Anyone who is sufficiently aware and sufficiently evolved even to wonder about whether they had lived before is certain to have done so. So, although it might take more than one attempt before you are relaxed enough for the past-life regression to be effective, you can be sure that there is something there just waiting for you to discover it.

[v]

WAYS OF EXPERIENCING
PAST-LIFE REGRESSION

We are all different, with our own unique combination of perceptions and beliefs, so we do not all experience a session of past-life regression in the same way. This does not mean that any one way of experiencing it is better than any other – there is no 'right' or 'wrong' in this process.

Some people, particularly those who have already had some experience of being hypnotized, are able to put themselves in the midst of the events of their past lives. They will say, 'I am doing this' or 'That is happening to me'. For others, this depth of involvement may not be possible, especially during a first or second session of regression – although the more they get used to the concept and the technique, the more deeply involved they may become.

Having said that, there are those for whom this will never be possible and these people should not feel that they are not responding as ably as others or that their previous existence has any less validity. These are the people who will talk about things happening to 'him' or 'her' – almost as though the person they are observing had nothing to do with them.

SEEING PICTURES

It has already been indicated that the ability to visualize is a great help when it comes to being regressed – but this mainly applies to the technique itself. Once in the past life, however, some people find it quite easy to see what is going on while others see nothing at all in their heads. As before, this does not mean that their past life is any less real; simply that they may have a certain amount of apprehension about the process and their ever-watchful subconscious mind is preventing them from seeing anything in case they find it distressing. Not being able to see images will not invalidate the regression session provided you keep an open mind and continue to communicate with the therapist. It is probable that, as you read this book, you know with certainty what you have on your feet – shoes, slippers, boots or, perhaps, nothing at all. You do not have to look at your feet to know this – it is simply a fact. In the same way, even if you do not see what is going on around you when you are being regressed, you will know what is happening and be able to describe it.

NAMES AND DATES

It is important to remember that no matter how engrossed you may become in the happenings of your former life, you never entirely lose the awareness of the present-day person you are. For this reason, the therapist will not usually ask you your name as a direct question because your instinct would be to give the one you have today.

The most common way of finding out the name of subjects revealed during a regression is to ask them to find something to write on and something to write with and then get them to write their name and see what appears. This usually has the desired result. If the person you were in a former life happens to have been illiterate, you will probably be asked to see someone you know coming towards you calling your name and to listen to what they call you.

There might be a problem in dealing with someone who was a peasant, a country dweller in early times or a recluse, because to people like this the date – even if they knew it – was unimportant. But, even if they cannot tell you the year, they will usually know which king or queen is on the throne. Even if they do not know the precise date, they will be aware of the season of the year.

Matthew

When Matthew was regressed to a previous life, he described a harsh existence unloading cargo from ships that arrived at Liverpool docks in the nineteenth century. When he was asked what a particular set of crates contained, he replied that he did not know – and, indeed, was not at all interested. All he was concerned about was unloading them and stacking them so that he could get his pay and go home. Wanting to probe further, I asked Matthew if there were any markings or writing on the crates. On being told that there were, I asked him what this writing said. Matthew replied that he did not know as he had never learned to decipher it. I put a pencil into Matthew's hand and put a piece of paper within his reach and asked him to write his own name. The result was a large and somewhat shaky cross.

THE DETACHMENT TECHNIQUE

Unlike some of the pioneers of past-life regression, most hypnotherapists these days take great care to ensure that their patients are not caused any suffering during a session – whether mental, physical or emotional. It is quite possible to do this using what is called the 'detachment technique', while still achieving the benefits required from the regression. Even today, however, there are still some hypnotherapists and counsellors who believe that, unless the pain and distress of a former traumatic situation is actually experienced by the subject, that person will not be able to overcome the problems this traumatic situation has gone on to cause in their present life. This is not true.

Indeed, it has recently been widely reported in the media that professional counsellors have now come to the conclusion that making someone repeatedly describe in detail a traumatic experience can actually increase that person's suffering rather than reduce it – something many of us have been saying for years. It might be advisable, therefore, should you decide to consult a hypnotherapist, to make certain that the one you have chosen to see is one who will take care to ensure that you do not experience any pain or distress during the course of your sessions. This applies whether you are dealing with problems that occurred in this life or in a past one.

THE CINEMA SCREEN

Imagine that you are watching an old movie of yourself when you were just ten years old. On the screen you see that the child you were then has fallen over. Perhaps you can see that, at that time, you grazed your knees quite badly, making them bleed; you may even have cried. Looking at that film now, you would know that, when you were ten, you experienced pain and you were unhappy – but your knees would not hurt today, nor would you feel any distress. The most you would experience is sympathy for the child you once were. This is how the detachment technique works. It should be explained to you before the session of hypnosis begins.

The hypnotherapist is experienced enough to judge (from the pattern of your breathing and the movement of your eyes behind the closed lids) when something distressing is about to occur, so he or she can remind you to detach yourself from the event and to observe it on that cinema screen inside your head.

Although the detachment technique ensures that you do not suffer any anguish, you may still feel some emotion. You might feel sorrow for the situation that the former 'you' is experiencing. If some form of unkindness is being perpetrated towards you, you will probably feel angry. But it will be the anger of the adult you are now on behalf of the person you once were. None of these emotions will be any greater than you might feel while watching a fictional film, when perhaps you might feel sad or even cry at some event portrayed on the screen. Similarly, we all feel anger when we see examples of cruelty or inhumanity on a cinema or television screen. It can be very helpful to experience this sort of emotion while detached from the actual event.

It may be that the person you were on that cinema screen did not understand the reason for the emotions felt at the time, whereas now that you are viewing the same situation from a distance you can see far more clearly. You will also be able to watch the progress of events as the regression unfolds and see whether the emotion was justified or whether, indeed, it was in some way responsible for a chain of events that followed. The anger sometimes experienced during a period of detachment can be very therapeutic in itself. Suppose the person you used to be was in some way vulnerable – a victim unable to defend him or herself. The common factor among such people is that they may experience all kinds of emotions at the time – fear, guilt, self-dislike, for example – but do not feel anger at the perpetrator. Being able to experience that anger at a later, more evolved, stage in your development can be helpful as it seems to finish off what was 'unfinished business'. The anger is on behalf of the vulnerable person (adult or child) that you once were and, having experienced it, you allow your inner child to grow and develop in a way that was prevented by that very vulnerability.

Some people, particularly when experiencing past-life regression for the first time, prefer to be a detached observer during the whole process as this gives them the confidence to know that nothing can possibly hurt them during the entire session. While this is not necessary, most hypnotherapists would be happy to allow the session to proceed in this way if it helped to give subjects greater confidence as they would find it much easier to relax and the hypnotic state would, therefore, be deeper.

FACT OR FICTION?

It is only natural that people should question whether what appear to be past life experiences are really so or whether they are simply figments of the imagination of the subject. That is just as it should be – questioning is always healthier than blind acceptance, whatever the theory. Any hypnotherapist who has worked for some time in the field of past-life regression will be able to tell you of cases where facts have arisen during a session that have later been researched and found to be true. I am not talking about facts that could have been known previously, because of something the person has seen or read in the past, for example, but of details that no one could have been aware of until corroborative research was carried out.

andrew

During the course of a past-life regression, Andrew, who lived in the north of England, told me of a life he had spent as a cloth merchant in and around the area of Bristol. He was able to give details of his name, the year, and the type of cloth he had sold. Some time later he contacted me again and said that, during a recent holiday, he had travelled to Bristol (an area he had not visited before) and had eventually found details of his former self on a parish register. Although the previous life lived by Andrew was not of itself particularly exciting, actually finding proof of this previous existence certainly was. The fact that this was a man unknown to history, about whom nothing had been written and no films had been made, meant that discovering those details was all the more fascinating.

WHEN REGRESSION IS INVENTION

Most hypnotherapists, even those who are firm believers in past lives and reincarnation, will accept that a certain number of 'regressions' are in fact creations of the imagination of the subject. It is not thought that this is a deliberate act on the part of the person seeking past-life regression – it would be a pointless and expensive exercise. But it is possible that the person concerned is looking for an answer and allows his or her imagination to create it. This is sometimes the case when someone is suffering from a current phobia. As a phobia is, by definition, an illogical fear, so the patient usually feels foolish for being terrified of something that most people are quite at ease with. That feeling of foolishness is, in itself, often sufficient to prevent a cure taking place. If such patients 'discover' that a previous life offers an explanation for their phobia, the feeling of foolishness is dispelled. Now they have a reason for their condition. Does it matter, in such a case, whether the past life situation really existed or whether the patient's subconscious mind invented it? The outcome is still the same. The feeling of foolishness disappears and it is possible for patient and therapist to go on together to work successfully on overcoming the phobia.

Even in cases where it might be suspected that the past-life regression is the product of the patient's imagination, there must be a reason why a person's subconscious mind comes up with a particular set of images and facts. Say the word 'house' to ten different people and each will see a different picture in their mind – based on their individual previous experiences, their likes and dislikes, their hopes and their fears. Those who believe in the development and evolvement of the individual spirit find it easy to accept that, even in cases that may be imagined, there is purpose and understanding in the supposed regression that is experienced.

CAN WE BE SURE?

However experienced we believe ourselves to be as hypnotherapists, we can never be entirely certain whether or not a particular past life is, in fact, the product of the subject's imagination. There are so many occasions when, even if the facts are absolutely true, they would be virtually impossible to research. For this reason it is wiser to treat each regression as a true example of a past life. We do not have the right to set ourselves up as judges of what is real and what is not.

Often the best 'proof' is what the subject feels inside. You will find that patients who have experienced a session of past-life regression usually know, deep within themselves, that they truly were another person living in another time.

WHO WERE YOU?

Even before their first session of past-life regression, most people are somewhat curious about the type of person they might have been — male/female; rich/poor; good/evil, and so on. It is important to understand that each of us has probably been all of these things as we progressed through our former lives. Some Eastern philosophies believe that, prior to becoming a human being, each person started off as a rock, then some sort of plant — usually a tree — before becoming a fish and then a mammal. They believe that it is only after living lives at each of these stages that we can become human.

It is not possible to prove for a fact whether this is so or not. But Western regression specialists — and, in particular, hypnotherapists who have the opportunity to question the person undergoing the regression — have found no evidence of an existence prior to the human one. This does not mean that most therapists do not believe that animals have spirits too — simply that animals become other animals while people become other people.

So, if we accept for the moment that you were always human, what sort of people have you been? Some are surprised to find that they have been both male and female in previous lives. Yet, if we accept that these existences are all part of the learning process, surely it can only be beneficial to have experienced life as both a male and a female. It is often felt that the truly evolved person of today has achieved that fine balance between their masculine and feminine sides and this may have been possible because of the experiences they have had living as both sexes in former lives.

More than one person about to have a past-life regression session has expressed concern that they may have done something terrible in a former life. The fact is that they probably have. Indeed, if they had reached a state of such perfection that they had nothing more to learn, they probably would not exist in human form today.

The vital point to remember is that the person you are today is not responsible for the mistakes of the person you were in a former life. That person has gone. It is only the spirit that lives on in you and, hopefully, however bad the former person was, the right lessons were learned and the spirit has now progressed.

suzanne

Suzanne experienced her first session of past-life regression while receiving ongoing therapy for claustrophobia. Once the therapy was complete, however, she expressed the desire to find out more about some of the other lives she might have lived in the past. What follows is information about the various lives Suzanne and I were able to uncover over the course of about twelve months (not in chronological order but in the order in which they were experienced).

1 A seventeenth-century nun who dared to express her disapproval of the way in which the convent was being run. As a punishment, she was confined to a solitary existence in a small cell with no window or link with the outside world.

2 A male convict who was sent to Australia as punishment for the theft of food for his family. He fared extremely well in that country, starting out by working as a labourer for a farmer and eventually owning a farm of his own.

3 A young woman in France in the early twentieth century who married a very wealthy man. Her husband set out to make a home for them overseas but, when she attempted to follow him, the ship in which she was sailing sank and she was drowned.

4 A Cromwellian foot-soldier who fought staunchly for his master and who held strong anti-royalist beliefs. This led him to behave in a very cruel fashion to those who opposed him.

5 A little girl in an Italian household who, although poor, lived a very happy life in the bosom of a large and loving family.

GOING BACKWARDS IN TIME

When hypnotherapists first began working with past-life regression, one of the methods they would employ for reaching a former life was to work backwards through the subject's current life and then still further back through the years prior to this until another incarnation was uncovered. This method has virtually disappeared today – for good reason.

It was found that this method could cause great distress to those undergoing regression. For one thing, they might have had a really unhappy time at some earlier period in their present life and so to take them back through this time might bring to the fore difficult or painful memories and emotions that would serve no useful purpose at all. Who is to know at the outset which of their previous lives was the traumatic and therefore unpleasant to experience? Perhaps the most recent former life was one in which terrible things happened that caused the former person great pain, whether physical or emotional. In such a case – particularly if this is the first attempt at past-life regression – the subconscious mind, which is so protective, might block out the memory completely because it feels that the person concerned is not yet ready and able to cope with it.

If this protective block does not occur and the life is examined in detail by subjects, they may experience something that distresses them. No ethical hypnotherapist ever sets out to hurt anyone in any way at all as this could cause problems for the present-day person. By allowing the subconscious mind to select for itself the life it wishes to examine on any particular occasion, both therapist and subject can feel confident that nothing will arise that would be painful or upsetting and that the subject would be unable to cope with.

When subjects are initially regressed to a former life, they may present themselves as being of any age. They might first be aware of themselves as a small child, a young man or woman, a mature person or someone who is very old.

Once they feel comfortable with that person, however, it is quite simple for the hypnotherapist to take them backwards or forwards in that particular life. Usually this is done by using a specific technique and then asking the subject to go backwards or forwards in that life for as few or as many years as their subconscious mind chooses and, when that stage is reached, to talk about where they are and what they are doing.

This method is used to avoid problems that might otherwise arise if the therapist was to choose a specific number of years for a subject to progress only to put them right in the middle of a painful or distressing experience. Also, because we do not know at the outset what age the former person was when he or she died, it avoids asking patients to go to a year when they no longer existed. As well as enabling the hypnotherapist to help subjects to experience different stages of a single life, the above method sometimes helps to prove to those being regressed that what they are experiencing is real and not imagined.

An Iranian man who lived and worked in the United Kingdom and who spoke perfect English was being regressed and, at first, described himself as a small boy in the African jungle, living with other members of his tribe. The existence was not a particularly happy one and at one point the child cried — tears rolled down the cheeks of the man himself. To avoid causing the man distress, I asked him to go on in that life for as many years as his subconscious mind chose. The man then described a period some fifteen years later when the troubled times were over and he was enjoying life. At the end of the regression the subject said that he was not surprised to find that actual tears had flowed as, even in the present life, he was a very emotional man who would cry at beautiful music or sad films. What had convinced him that he was really engrossed in a former life was that moments later (when he had progressed fifteen years) the tears and the emotion that had accompanied them had completely disappeared. As anyone who cries easily will know, it is not possible simply to 'turn off' tears in that way, even when the reason for them no longer exists. But for this man, because in his mind fifteen years had elapsed, the reason for the tears was so far in the past that no trace remained of them or the emotion he felt at that time.

Among the common factors found in by far the majority of cases of past-life regression is that we usually encounter people whom we are able to recognize from our present life, even though the relationship and circumstances that exist around this encounter may be totally different.

The commonly held theory regarding reincarnation and relationships is that we seem to pass through life after life surrounded by the same nuclear circle of people. There will also, of course, be any number of other individuals who play a fleeting part in our lives or who appear only briefly, never to be seen again. If we accept this theory, it becomes easy to understand how we can meet somebody on one occasion and know without doubt that we have found a friend, while someone else, whom we may have known for years, will never progress beyond being an acquaintance. In the former case there is some sort of mutual recognition that does not exist with the latter person.

This may also explain why we feel instinctively that we do not care for an individual, even though that person – in this lifetime – has never done anything untoward or upset us in any way. Somewhere deep in the subconscious mind, the memory of an ancient dislike, has been triggered. Having said that, in many cases this instinctive dislike or distrust disappears as we get to know the present-day person and that inner memory appears to fade.

This could also explain seemingly unreasonable prejudices, such as someone declaring that they do not like people from a certain country or region. Perhaps the person they used to be suffered at the hands of that country in a previous life and, although the memory has faded, the prejudice has remained.

It is interesting to note the many different roles one person can play in a series of previous lives. The person who is your father today may have been your sister in one past life, your child in another and, in yet another, your best friend or your chief enemy. We appear to need to experience different relationships with the same person throughout many lives in order to complete the pattern.

Some astrologers also claim that we ourselves need to have experienced being born under each birth sign during our series of lifetimes. This, however, is often difficult to establish as, until comparatively recently, there were many places where dates of birth were not recorded and so, even if successfully regressed, subjects were quite unable to state with accuracy when they were born.

One woman spoke of being born in a peasant village in Russia in the middle of the nineteenth century but had no idea at all of the actual date of her birth. All she could say with certainty was that there was thick snow on the ground.

You might wonder how, if people who are close to us appear in different roles in our different lives, we are able to recognize them as the people we know now. Yet this does not appear to present a problem. The recognition is obviously not by superficial appearance alone but by some deep inner 'eye' that looks beyond the outward view.

Diana

When Diana was being regressed to a former life, she said that she was a widow with three young daughters to support, one of whom had a deformed leg and needed extra attention. At the end of the regression she told me that she had recognized that this crippled child was, in fact, her boyfriend John in her present life. She found it quite amusing as, apart from the fact that he was over six feet tall and extremely fit, John had a bushy ginger beard – quite unlike the fragile little girl of the earlier life. Yet Diana had no doubt whatsoever that they were one and the same spirit.

Sometimes it seems that we are meant to learn from the progressive relationships we have with a single individual. If we have hurt them – or been hurt by them – in a former life, we may become more sensitive towards them this time. If we have loved them deeply in the past that love seems to grow even deeper in the current lifetime. If we have disliked them or been prejudiced against them in a previous existence, perhaps we are being given the opportunity in this life to show that we have learned from our mistakes and will not behave in the same way again. The opportunities to learn these lessons are put before us – it is up to us how well we succeed.

THE DEATH EXPERIENCE

In many cases, hypnotherapists will take their subjects through the end of the previous life, if this seems appropriate, to let them observe what comes afterwards. This is a perfectly safe process that need cause no pain, discomfort or distress to those experiencing it. The techniques and words used to achieve this may vary slightly from therapist to therapist but the basic method remains very much the same.

Firstly, the therapist will remind subjects that they can detach themselves at any time from what is happening in the former life and watch it on that huge movie screen in their mind. Then they will be taken to the last day of that life and asked to describe it in any way they wish. It will usually become obvious whether this is a gentle passing of a sick or elderly person or whether death is premature and brought about by some violent means.

Subjects will then be asked to slip through the end of that life to whatever comes after it and to tell the therapist what, if anything, they are aware of. It is interesting that – almost without exception – people give very much the same sort of description as the life comes to an end. One might perhaps expect that those with some knowledge of spiritualism or who have a deeply held religious belief would speak about what comes next in similar words – but even those who have no such knowledge use almost identical terms.

The first point of importance is that, after death, there appears to be no pain at all. In fact, if there was pain in the time leading up to death, it disappears as the life ends. There is sometimes sadness, as in the case of a woman who (in her former life) died while her children were still young. She was understandably sad that she would not be there with them as they grew up.

Most people describe the immediate feeling as one of warmth and lightness, coupled with a sense of joyful anticipation, even if they are not quite sure what it is that they are looking forward to. Many speak of travelling through a dark place – some call it a cave, others a tunnel – towards the light. And it is this light that they are anxious to reach. Once they do, they speak of intense light and varied colours. One woman told me that she was surrounded by beautiful colours and, when I asked her what colours they were, she replied that she could not tell me as we, in our present lives, do not have words for the colours she was seeing.

Through the light there appears a figure – sometimes more than one. This happens on almost every occasion. Even when the figure does not appear, the person being taken through the experience somehow knows that they are about to do so.

Some people describe this figure in almost religious terms – a holy person, or someone in robes, for example. Others say that it is their father, their grandmother, or some other person they have known during the course of the lifetime they have just been experiencing. Sometimes there is more than one figure but, even when this is so, there is one predominant person who it seems will help the person who has died on to the next stage in their journey.

When subjects are brought out of hypnosis and talk about the past-life regression and, in particular, the death experience, they often feel greatly comforted by the fact that what follows this life seems to be both pleasant and comfortable. Even more importantly, most find it reassuring to know – and they do know – that they will not have to continue on their way alone. For, if someone came to meet them after each of their previous lives, there is no reason to suppose that this will not happen when their current life comes to an end.

Of course, however many theories there may be about what happens to our spirit after we die, no one can state that they are a 100 per cent certain about what will take place. But because all these people, whatever their backgrounds, beliefs and previous knowledge, seem to have very much the same experiences, with only slight variations, it makes it easier to believe that this must be what will happen to each of us.

If subjects tell the therapist from the outset – or when it is suggested to them – that they do not wish to go through the death experience then, of course, they will not have to do so. They might, however, be missing out on a very powerful lesson that could give them great comfort.

[VI]

REMOVING BLOCKS

Whether we are dealing with present or past lives, it is possible to remember things while in a state of hypnosis that we have otherwise forgotten. Sometimes these are things that, once we recall them, we say of them, 'Oh, yes – I remember that'. At other times we may have no conscious memory of them at all.

Your subconscious mind never forgets anything. It is able to retain everything you have ever seen, heard or done. When you are hypnotized, the therapist is able to help you to access your subconscious mind and its memories, so you can bring to the forefront of your mind all those incidents and experiences that your conscious mind has long since forgotten.

Think of it as a giant filing system inside your head. How easily you are able to retrieve a piece of information from any filing system often depends, firstly, on how accurately you filed it in the first place and, secondly, on how vast a system you have to go through in order to find what you want.

The older you are and the more experiences you have had, the greater the number of pieces of information in your internal filing system. This would explain why we cannot possibly remember everything all the time – our minds would be such a jumble of thoughts and details that we would never be able to think clearly.

The same applies to memories of former lives. Think how difficult it would be to spend each day with our minds full of memories from several different lifetimes. This does not mean that we are not able to access these memories when we choose to, and when we set about doing so methodically – but it does help us to understand why, for the greater part of the time, those recollections remain firmly entrenched in our inner filing system.

BLOCKED MEMORIES

In our current life, there may be experiences that we have chosen to block from our memory – storing them in the most hidden recesses of that filing system so that we cannot come upon them unintentionally. Sometimes that blocking is done deliberately; perhaps the memory is too painful and would cause us too much distress if we brought it to mind. At other times, even though we did not decide to block a particular memory, the subconscious mind (which is always acting as your protector) may have made that decision for you, deciding that you were not yet ready to look at that specific part of your past again.

Your subconscious mind will go on protecting you in this way, even during a session of hypnosis. No one can be forced to recall something that the subconscious mind does not feel he or she is ready to re-experience. So you need have no fear that, under hypnosis, you will be forced to confront past demons that you would prefer to leave buried.

Of course, if you are having hypnosis as part of therapy, one of the reasons you will be doing so is that you wish to overcome whatever problems you may have. Even if that includes looking at things hitherto blocked from your mind, the subconscious mind will feel that it has your permission to retrieve the relevant information, provided you trust your therapist, he or she has explained to you about the detachment technique so that you know you cannot re-experience hurt, and you are keen to overcome your current problem.

Mandy

When Mandy was forty years old, she was returning one evening from a visit to a friend when she was dragged into a nearby alley and raped at knifepoint. Her attacker made his escape but Mandy was able to give a full description when questioned by the police. A man was arrested and a trial date was set.

As so often happens, it was many months before the trial was to take place and in that time Mandy blocked the memory of those horrifying events from her mind. However, she was the only witness; if she was unable to recall those events at the trial, the man would go free.

Two years prior to the attack, Mandy had consulted me in order to give up smoking – which she had done successfully. Now she came to see me again and I was able, while giving her the protection of the detachment technique, to help her remember what had happened and also to see again in her mind the face of the man who had raped her. This happened because Mandy herself wanted it. She was determined that the man should go to prison for what he had done so that other women might be spared what she had experienced. As a result of Mandy's testimony, her attacker was sentenced to seven years in prison.

DÉJÀ VU

Many people have had experiences of déjà vu when they feel they already know a place or a person and yet are also aware that they have never been to that spot or encountered that person before in their lives. Déjà vu is often put forward as proof that the individual has lived before and it was during that life that the original encounter took place. But you will also have heard the theory that déjà vu is not the result of having lived a past life. It is said that when we get a sense of having been somewhere before, what is really happening is that we are simply dredging up from the depths of our memory something that we have seen, heard or read earlier in our current life.

Thanks to television, cinema and illustrated books, it is probable that many cases of so-called déjà vu can be put down to a simple case of recognizing something one has consciously forgotten having seen in the past. This does not mean to imply that anyone experiencing déjà vu is either deliberately lying or is foolish for not being able to remember that past experience. Think, for example, of someone watching an adventure film at the cinema. He may be so engrossed in the plot that he fails to consciously take in the building or street name in the background of a particular scene. However, the subconscious absorbs everything and stores it deep within the mind. So, when the person actually comes upon that place in real life in the future, the subconscious is able to bring the image to the forefront of their mind and, when they are able to know in advance what is just around the corner, they accept it as an example of genuine déjà vu.

Tommy

Tommy was just three years old when his parents took him to visit an aunt living in a town about twenty miles from their home. Not having a car, the family travelled by coach to the edge of the town and then, descending, had to find the way to the aunt's house on foot.

As the father and mother studied the street map, Tommy informed them that to get to where they wanted to go they had to walk down the hill, past the church, over the bridge and across the park. Looking at the map, his parents saw to their amazement that the little boy was quite right.

Tommy had never been to this town before. He was unable to read so could not have studied the map in advance. He could not have heard his parents discussing the route as, until they left the coach, they had no idea of which way they were to go. How could Tommy have known the details of the route so accurately unless he had been there before in some former life?

It is interesting to note here that Tommy did not use any place names (which frequently change) when describing the route to be taken but spoke of landmarks that would have been unchanged for generations.

DÉJÀ VU OF A PERSON

This form of déjà vu is slightly different and far more difficult to prove. There are so many people in the world who bear a resemblance to someone else that it is possible to claim that each experience of 'recognizing' someone is in reality just a sign that the brain has picked up on one or more of that person's features, compared them with those of someone you have seen earlier in this life, and decided that the two people are one and the same.

In fact, when it comes to true recognition of someone whom your spirit has known in a previous life, physical recognition is usually the last thing to be taken into account – especially when you realize that the person may have changed size, colouring and even sex since that last encounter.

SYNCHRONICITY

Synchronicity is a term coined by the Swiss psychiatrist Carl Jung. It refers to significant happenings that have no apparent cause but which have a considerable effect upon the person or people concerned. A case of being in the right place at the right time for something that you desire to take place – even though you might think of it as a 'lucky break'. Jung also used the word to include such occurrences as precognitive dreaming, omens and déjà vu.

Scientists explain synchronicity as a matter of combining the information contained in the two hemispheres of the brain. Those who believe in reincarnation might claim that it is proof of having lived before or of having spiritual protective powers that work for our own good. Although almost impossible to prove, it is likely that there are cases where either of these may be the true explanation.

GROUP REGRESSION

Some people who might feel a little apprehensive about experiencing a session of past-life regression may decide to start with group regression. They feel more secure when surrounded by a circle of friends and, although the experience is different from that of an individual regression, they can still derive considerable benefit from it. Obviously, a group regression is quite different from one that is experienced by a single individual. For one thing, it should never be undertaken as part of ongoing therapy, which is an intensely personal and confidential process. Group regressions are for those who are curious about their past lives and are 'dipping a toe in the water' of the experience of discovery. There are major differences in the experience, some may pose difficulties and some can prove beneficial.

The difficulties

- Although the group will consist of no more than six to eight people, as a greater number would be difficult to handle, it is obviously more difficult for the therapist to give full attention to each and every person present. For this reason, the regressions will usually be on a lighter level than those undertaken by individuals and it may, therefore, mean that former lives are observed more superficially.
- Whereas, during an individual regression, the information is elicited by the questions of the therapist and the responses of the subject, this is naturally not possible with several people in the room. If they all spoke at once there would be a meaningless babble and, in any event, the same questions would not apply to all of them.
- It is possible that one member of the group may find it more difficult than the others to relax and enter the hypnotic state. During an individual session, the therapist can pause at this point – perhaps repeating and reinforcing the initial induction – but if this were to be done during a group session, the others, who had already been hypnotized, might begin to come out of that state and therefore be unable to regress when the time came.
- It is not possible to ask specific questions of individual people in a group setting, so the therapist has to be more vague and suggest that all the group members observe and remember what is happening around them. Some people, particularly those who are not used to hypnosis, may find this more difficult than others and the depth of their attention may therefore lapse.
- Just as in this lifetime, the length of each person's past life will vary and so one person may have completed the experience while the others are still discovering what happened during their particular previous incarnation.
- If one member of the group is restless and shifts position frequently – or perhaps coughs loudly – this can distract the others present and make it more difficult for them to concentrate fully on the regression.

The benefits

- When several people in the same room are deliberately assisted to the state of deep relaxation required for hypnosis, an aura of tranquillity may pervade the room. This can be of great help to those who may be finding relaxation a little more difficult to achieve.

• Those who are nervous about the whole process may derive great comfort from the fact that the others in the room are undergoing a similar experience to themselves.

• In the majority of cases, there is already a link between the people in the room – friends, family, neighbours, members of a shared-interest group, for example – so it is often found that they will encounter some of these people during a previous life experience and this will add to the depth of their knowledge.

conclusion

While it must be remembered that group regression should never be undertaken as part of individual therapy, it can be of great interest and benefit to those who take part. Even when entered into because of simple curiosity, the experience may well be responsible for opening a door to the greater development and evolvement of the people concerned.

SHARED INFORMATION

It is not uncommon for two friends or two members of the same family to find common links in their previous lives. And this is the case even when there has been absolutely no opportunity for discussion or collusion between the people concerned. This is even more evident when a group regression session is conducted.

It should not seem surprising that two participants in a group regression session should find that there was a link between them in one or more of their previous lives because, as we have already seen, those who mean a great deal to us in one lifetime usually play a significant role in many others.

However, one also has to consider the theory that because all those being regressed are in the same room and because they are in the 'altered state' of hypnosis (which is akin to the meditative state), there is a possibility that some sort of thought transference may be taking place. If one or more of the participants has strong psychic tendencies, they may well be receiving information from one of the others present.

While it is not possible to disprove such a theory, most people who have had a past-life regression claim that they have absolutely no doubt that what they experienced was truly a glimpse of one of their own previous incarnations. It is almost impossible to explain this feeling to anyone who has not yet been regressed, but subjects usually know with complete certainty that they were not dreaming and that what they saw, heard and felt was not simply a figment of their imagination.

Angie and Donald

Angie had been responsible for organizing a group of friends and family who were to have a past-life-regression session together. A few days before the event was due to take place, one member of the group had to withdraw owing to ill health. Unable to find anyone else at such short notice, Angie persuaded her husband Donald to make up the numbers. Donald agreed somewhat reluctantly as he was not sure that he even believed in the concept of past lives.

Before the start of the session, Donald explained to me just how he felt and asked what he should do. I said that it would be perfectly all right for him to take part as long as he remained open-minded and waited to see what happened. At the very worst, even if no past life showed itself, Donald would experience a very pleasant period of deep relaxation.

When the session was over, Donald rushed from the room and returned clutching pen and paper. While the other members of the group were discussing what they had experienced, he remained in his chair, silently drawing on his pad. Angie talked of a past life as the captain of an English ship during the era of Queen Elizabeth I. This captain had been a stern but fair man who showed great concern for the wellbeing of his crew. In particular, he had a soft spot for a young boy who worked on the ship.

At this point Donald interrupted to say that he had, in fact, been a powder monkey on an Elizabethan vessel. He was a small boy whose job it was to fetch the gunpowder needed for the heavy guns carried by the ship. The picture he had so carefully drawn was of the rigging of that ship and it was extremely detailed, even showing the types of knots used to secure the rigging. During the course of his regression Donald recognized the captain as Angie, his current wife.

Some time later, I received a letter from Angie and Donald who had taken the time and trouble to investigate the design of ships of the Elizabethan period and, in particular, their rigging. It turned out that Donald's drawing depicted a style of rigging that was in use at that time. This was made all the more interesting by the fact that, in his present life, Donald had no knowledge — and indeed no interest — in ships of any sort, past or present, yet his drawing had been correct in every detail.

It was also interesting to note that Angie (who, in that earlier life, had taken such good care of the lad Donald had been) had suffered from poor health for a considerable amount of time in her current life. Donald had taken time off work to stay at home and care for her, looking after her with love and tenderness until she was fully recovered. Perhaps he was repaying a debt from all those years ago.

HOW A GROUP REGRESSION IS CONDUCTED

As you would imagine, a group session is run in a quite different way from that in which an individual regression session is conducted. In most cases a group regression takes several hours — sometimes it is a complete one-day workshop — whereas an individual session usually lasts little more than one hour.

Many of the people who attend a group regression have little or no knowledge of how hypnosis works or what it feels like, and therefore no experience of regression. The first part of the day, therefore, is usually taken up with an explanation by the therapist of what to expect when being hypnotized. This may be followed by a short session of light hypnosis — with no mention at all of regression or past lives — to allow people present to experience the sensation. After this they will be given time to ask any general questions about hypnosis that they might have.

Next will come an explanation and discussion on the concept of past lives. The hypnotherapist will tell everyone present exactly what the rest of the day's programme will involve — what the hypnotherapist will do, what they should expect, and so on. This also gives everyone a chance to voice any doubts or fears that they may have so that their minds can be set at rest. As in Donald's case, they will usually be told that the worst that can occur is that nothing of significance will happen and they will have no past life experience. (This is more likely to occur because of some apprehension on their part, rather than because they do not actually have a past life to tune into.) In that case they should just enjoy the deep relaxation and feelings of relief from stress that they will experience.

Then comes the regression session itself. Although the induction technique is the same as for an individual regression, what follows will be different. Instead of asking questions, waiting for replies and then asking further questions based on those replies, the hypnotherapist suggests that everyone observes what is happening around them, notices what is important and remembers it so that it can be discussed afterwards.

Once the past life experience is over, the group members are brought out of hypnosis. They are then encouraged to talk about what they felt during the regression. This is even more important in a group situation than it would be when dealing with an individual. For one thing, the individual will be given a cassette of the questions and answers during their session so they will have a permanent record of what took place. For another, it is interesting to note how many links there may be between the lives and experiences of the people in the group.

If this is a full one-day workshop, there is then an interval for people to stretch their legs, get a little fresh air or have refreshment before starting another past life session. The interval is intended to be more than a social moment; it is essential for the subjects to be able to put one past life to one side before experiencing another and so avoid confusion in their minds when they come to think about each life afterwards.

As there is no audio cassette for each person to take away afterwards, they will be encouraged to write down what they can remember as soon as possible. This is partly because it is easy for details to slip from the memory once we return to our everyday lives, and partly because further information about a specific past life will often come unbidden into the mind for some time after the original experience – and unless the original facts have been noted, it would be all too easy to confuse which facts are part of which previous life.

During the course of a group regression, the therapist regularly reminds members of the detachment technique and of the fact that they will not experience pain or distress. This is because it is not possible to watch several people as closely as one can observe an individual and it is necessary to ensure that no one suffers in any way at any time.

It is also quite usual to have gentle music playing in the background during a group regression. This is not always the case when an individual session is taking place. Although the music should not be intrusive, its presence often serves to disguise small noises, such as someone shifting position or coughing, which might otherwise be a distraction.

All things considered, a group regression can be an excellent way for someone who is a little nervous to try something different in the company of people they trust. In the majority of cases it seems to lead to a desire for the more detailed type of information that can only be gleaned from an individual session of past-life regression.

fOLLOWING UP INfORMATION

It is always interesting when someone who has experienced a past-life regression session decides to carry out some research afterwards in order to check, as far as possible, any facts that may have come to light during the session. This is even more useful when a group regression session has taken place.

For most people – particularly those who are currently in a loving relationship or who are good friends – the discovery that they have known each other and interacted together in one or more of their past lives can be a very moving experience. When there is someone who is special to us, we all like to feel that our relationship with them transcends the mundane. The fact that we may have known them in previous incarnations helps us to believe that this is so.

Of course, it is also possible to encounter during past-life regression someone with whom you have had an unhappy relationship in your current life. Even this can be beneficial. Sometimes it is possible to see how events in this life amount to completing the 'unfinished business' of the former one.

Justine

Justine was in her mid-thirties when she had a session of past-life regression. During the former life she stated that she was a young male athlete living in northern Italy. She had a brother who was also athletic and with whom she was fiercely competitive. She described the way in which she would often cheat in order to win when competing with her brother – whether in sport or in life in general.

In her current life, when Justine was twenty-four and beginning to make a name for herself in the field of marketing, she met and married a young man who worked in the same type of job. A time came when, although still in love with one another, each had an exciting career offer that would necessitate a move to another part of the country. Unfortunately, these two regions were far apart. Each young person was ambitious and stubborn and refused to give up such excellent prospects in order to accompany the other to another area. Eventually Justine's husband left her in order to take up his new position and the marriage came to an end.

After her regression, Justine, who was by now happily married to someone else, felt that the problem with her first husband was a completion of the situation that arose all those years ago between the two young brothers in Italy.

KARMA

The laws of Karma – believed by some but not by others – state that there is always a price to pay for wrongdoing, even if it is paid in a future life.

Karma does not literally follow the concept of 'an eye for an eye and a tooth for a tooth', in that the retribution may take a completely different form from the original fault. To use an extreme example, someone who committed a murder in a previous life will not necessarily suffer at the hands of a murderer in this one. Perhaps they will be the mother of a murder victim and have to suffer the emotional upset this brings.

No one can be certain whether Karma exists or not but, if it does, it takes away the need for vengeance on the part of any individual as fate – even if it is in a future life – will exact its own punishment.

A MEETING OF SPIRITS

Most hypnotherapists who conduct group regression sessions can tell of at least one experience where two members of the group who are a couple seem to have defeated all the odds in order to be together. Perhaps there was parental objection, or perhaps life seemed to send them in different directions – and yet they still managed to end up together.

Invariably, such a couple will have known each other in several past incarnations, although possibly in a different type of loving relationship – perhaps as mother and child. Many times it can be found that, for any number of different reasons, the relationship in those past lives was ripped apart and the two people were forced to live separately from one another. Having experienced this situation for themselves during the course of their past-life regressions, the couple are often brought even closer together by the knowledge that they were obviously meant to be united and have now achieved this aim.

Such a relationship is often known as a meeting of 'twin souls' or 'twin spirits' and you will find that, even before they have been regressed to past lives, the couple know on some deep instinctive level that they have to be together.

[VII]

WHAT HAS MADE YOU THE WAY YOU ARE?

Each of us is the product not only of our genes and inherited characteristics but of the people we have encountered and the experiences we have had during our lifetime. This is even more true when we consider the spirit, travelling through many lifetimes and acquiring a different set of experiences in each. It is easy to understand how those who come from a troubled family background may have been adversely affected by their upbringing. But, even when all has gone smoothly, there will be differences within a single family.

You have probably heard a parent say that, having had (for example) three sons, and brought them all up the same way, they cannot understand why one should have turned out to be so different from the others. But it is impossible to bring up three sons in the same way. Only one has been the first child – and therefore, for a while, an only child. In the early stages of that child's life, the father and mother are still learning to be parents – they may be somewhat more protective and have more time to spend with their first child.

The second son is the only one to have been a middle child and possibly to feel that he can never catch up with his elder brother. His parents may feel more at ease with him because they now know how to look after a baby but, because they already have a toddler, they may also have less time to spend with him. At the same time, the older child may feel jealous or put out because so much of his mother's time now seems to be taken up with this new baby.

When the third son comes along it affects all three. The former 'only' child now has two rivals for his parents' attention. The second son is no longer the baby of the family and the youngest one himself – particularly if the parents have decided that this will be their last child – may be spoiled a little by father and mother.

So, with the same parents, the same financial and emotional background and the same practical opportunities, those three boys have, in fact, had three quite different experiences of childhood.

Add to the considerations already mentioned the fact that each person reacts differently to a similar situation and you will see how, even when there has been no terrible trauma to deal with, each of us is changed by what we experience. Two children in the same family may suffer from a childhood ailment such as chicken pox. One may have it quite mildly so that he is able to enjoy the enforced stay at home while he is in quarantine; the other might feel so unwell that he is confined to bed for the greater part of the time and suffers far more discomfort while the spots are healing. So the experience itself and the effect it has upon each child may be quite different.

If all that is true when we consider the events of a current life, it must apply to an even greater extent when considering a series of past lives. It may be that, as in many cases, the past lives of certain individuals were comparatively non-eventful, with those people living their various lifespans in an 'ordinary' way with no vividly traumatic events having taken place. Nonetheless, the fact of having been born in different eras, sometimes rich and sometimes poor, must make a difference to the effect that particular lives have had upon the spirit of the person concerned.

If, as is widely believed, our spirit chooses each of our earthly lives with the express intention of learning something important and thereby aiding our personal evolvement, it should be no surprise to us that we have to have all these different experiences. And the best thing any of us can do is to try to glean the required knowledge from each of those lives and take it forward on our spiritual journey.

The fact that, whatever your current beliefs, you have taken the time and trouble to read this book would indicate that you are a person with a reasonably evolved spirit. If this were not the case, you would have no desire to seek extra knowledge but would content yourself with the mundane and the material.

THE EFFECTS OF THE PAST

Just as each of us may be dramatically affected by what we have experienced in the earlier stages of this life, so we are all affected by what took place in our previous incarnations. This applies to good experiences as well as bad. We are also deeply affected by the people we have met and our own interactions with them, particularly when we realize that we are still interacting with those same people, albeit in different relationships.

Every single thing that has happened to us during the course of our past lives – whether good or bad – has affected us in some way or other. Starting from the basis of the human beings we were, with our positive and negative aspects and therefore our own different reactions to events, we have either learned or failed to learn something from each of these events.

Suppose, for example, that in a past life you had been dishonest and cheated a trusting friend out of money or position. In that life you might have carried on as normal without regard to what you had done, suffering no pangs of conscience at all. Or you might have spent the rest of your days tormented by feelings of guilt for your misdeeds. The way in which you reacted – that is, the way the human being you were chose to react – will have affected the remainder of that life and the lessons learned by the inner spirit. This, in turn, will have affected the choices made before the next incarnation. If the remorse had been genuine and the lesson learned, there might be an entirely new set of joys and woes for the new person to experience. But, if the earlier lesson had been ignored and nothing gained from the events of the previous life, then the person newly incarnated would be faced with similar opportunities (although they might present themselves in a different guise) the next time.

OTHER PEOPLE'S INFLUENCE

The people we encounter have a greater influence on our lives than we sometimes realize. Think of the person, adult or child, who is regularly belittled by someone with whom they have frequent contact – perhaps they are called 'stupid' or their ideas are regularly treated as ridiculous. However sensible or intelligent that person might be, the effect of hearing those words, day in and day out, can lead them to think of themselves as though they were indeed 'stupid' or their ideas 'ridiculous'.

This also applies when considering previous lives. If, in one lifetime, you were a man who was looked up to by all around him, who was considered to be wise and powerful, you would have lived in a way that was created by the acceptance of those beliefs. If, however, you had been looked down upon, treated as an inferior person or even completely ignored, your opinion of yourself would have been quite different. You could have been the same person, made different only by the words and actions of those around him.

The people who have such influences upon us are not necessarily bad or unkind. Sometimes they may be so caring, so eager to make life easy for you, that it becomes impossible for you to learn to stand on your own two feet. But whatever their motives, their effect upon you will still be considerable.

FEARS

Ongoing fears, in past lives or the present one, can be caused initially by events or by people. It is quite easy to understand how someone who was badly bitten by a ferocious dog can become nervous when approached by dogs in general. But such fears can also be passed on, from person to person. The sons and daughters of the bitten person may subconsciously sense the fear in their parent and, because children regard their parents as wise, all-knowing beings, may react with fear themselves.

A fear or phobia in the present life never remains static but always grows worse if nothing is done to deal with it – and the same applies to the period covering a series of lifetimes. A person bitten by a wild dog many centuries ago may well have died as a result of the injury, owing to the lack of adequate medical treatment at the time. This could have resulted in that person, in his next incarnation, being born with the fear of being bitten by a dog. If nothing is done to help him overcome that fear in the new life – or, even worse, if events during that life serve to increase or reinforce that fear – the person will take forward an even greater terror into his subsequent life.

If comparatively simple events, such as being bitten by a dog, can have this sort of effect, how much greater can be the effects of severe physical, mental or emotional happenings during a particular lifetime. The joy of working with past-life regression is that such tendencies can be recognized and work can be done to put them in the past for ever.

PRESENT LIFE REGRESSION

As already seen, past-life regression is frequently used as therapy to help someone overcome a problem they are facing in today's world, but it is not always necessary to delve so deeply (although it can never do any harm to do so). In some cases regression to an earlier stage in the current life is sufficient to discover the root cause of the problem. Whichever method is used, the follow-up technique is very much the same.

All ethical hypnotherapists take pains to ensure that their subjects start and leave their present-life regression with a good feeling. It may be the memory of a pleasant event or an enjoyable feeling. Even those who have very few good memories to look back upon will usually have had a favourite toy, which they found comforting, or a hiding place, in which they felt safe – and they will be asked to focus on this as they enter and leave the hypnotic state. Having reached the stage in their life in which the cause of their problem began, the same sort of question-and-answer session between therapist and subject takes place during regression into the present life as during a past-life regression. The person will be speaking in the voice and with the vocabulary of the age they have now reached, but the feelings will be those of the child they once were. In many cases, this can form part of the key to the solution to the problem. Consider how those things that seemed so enormously important to us when were five... nine... or fifteen years old are now things that we can look back on as being really trivial and you can see how a feeling could get 'stuck' in the subconscious mind so that we continue to experience it inwardly as if we were the age at which it happened, allowing it to grow out of all proportion.

moira

Moira was a young Irish Catholic woman who had been married for nearly two years. Ever since her marriage she had suffered from what she thought of as her 'fits'. They were not fits in the medical sense but severe panic attacks that left her feeling sick, dizzy and near to fainting. Because of these attacks she was frightened to become pregnant – which, as a devout Catholic wife, she felt was her duty. She feared that if she had an attack while pregnant, she might miscarry or injure her unborn child in some way. She was also afraid that even if she did manage to have a healthy child, she might have an attack while holding it, and so might drop and injure the baby.

When Moira was regressed, she went back to a time when she was four years old, the youngest child in a family of eight living in Ireland. Her parents had not had a great deal of money but no one went without the bare necessities and the family was a happy and loving one.

One day, when all the other children were at school, Moira was in the garden watching her mother hang the clothes on the washing line. In the manner of youngest children, she asked her mother if she could have a baby brother or sister. Without thinking, her mother replied 'Good gracious, no. It nearly killed me having you.'

Now this was not true. Moira's birth had not been particularly difficult. And her mother was not an unkind woman and certainly did not intend to frighten her youngest child – indeed Moira herself did not feel afraid at that time. All that happened was that, unthinkingly, her mother had used a silly phrase that many others have also used without meaning it to be taken literally. But, somewhere in the subconscious mind of that little girl, a link was formed between the concepts of childbirth and dying.

By the time the girl had grown up she had completely forgotten the original incident and, even had she remembered it, her logic would have reassured her that it was not true. But the subconscious had not forgotten the words and it had created Moira's panic attacks in order to give her an excuse not to have children

– and therefore not to die.

Once the cause of the problem was discovered and understood, it took no more than three sessions of hypnotherapy for a cure to take place. Moira became completely free of the debilitating panic attacks and went on to become the happy mother of three healthy sons.

REMOVING THE BLOCKS

It does not matter whether patients are able to remember the cause of their current problem but unable to do anything about it or whether they have grown up blocking the original cause completely from their mind. In either case the solution lies in regression because the subconscious mind never forgets anything and is able to bring it to the fore again. This time, however, the person is able to learn how to see the situation from the viewpoint of the adult they are now rather than the impressionable child they used to be.

VICTIM SYNDROME

There is a saying, 'Once a victim, always a victim' meaning that someone who is put upon by one person is all the more easily put upon by others too. It is worth looking at why this should be so and what, if anything, can be done to break the pattern. More often than not the original victimization takes place during our very early years. As children we are brought up to believe that adults in general – and our parents in particular – know far more than we do and are usually right. In many cases that is true, but what if one of those adults is an inadequate individual who is only able to feel powerful when acting against those who are unable to fight back? This can result in the adult making children into victims – either by means of verbal aggression or bullying or even by physically or sexually abusing them.

Children, not being in a position to fight back, experience many different negative emotions – guilt, inadequacy, inferiority, and so on. The one emotion they do not experience is anger – after all, adults are always right, aren't they? If the adult is right, children must be in the wrong and therefore deserving of the aggression shown towards them. Or so children think. And so they grow up with an inner sense of their own inferiority.

Even when such children become adults, can see and understand much more of the world around them and realize that the person who treated them badly was really in the wrong and had no right to act in such a way, that feeling of inferiority does not leave. It is firmly entrenched in the subconscious mind and, because of this, no amount of conscious logical thought is going to displace it.

Unless people who have grown up with this sense of inadequacy do something consciously to overcome it – usually best achieved with professional help – they will continue to reinforce the pattern by seeking out other people who treat them in the same way.

elizabeth

When she was ten years old, Elizabeth was sexually assaulted by a friend of her father's. It only happened on one occasion and she never told anyone about it, although the event had affected her personality in a negative way, causing her to lose her trust in people in general – and men in particular.

When she grew up, the adult Elizabeth was well able to see that what the man had done to her was a terrible thing and that she, as a child, had been in no way to blame. Yet she seemed to enter into one relationship after another with men who ended up treating her badly in some way. One was an alcoholic who would push her around when he was drunk. Another was a physically violent man while the third was verbally aggressive, calling Elizabeth terrible names and using violent and threatening language.

Eventually Elizabeth came to see me seeking help. With some assistance, she was able to see how she herself was continuing the pattern by subconsciously seeking out men who would turn her into a victim, although each had a different way of doing so. An intelligent woman, she naturally did not want this on a conscious level but, given a battle between the conscious and subconscious minds, the subconscious will always win.

In Elizabeth's subconscious mind, where the seed had been sown all those years ago, she was someone who 'deserved' to be treated as an inferior being – to be made into a victim. Indeed, if she had met a man who had insisted on putting her on a pedestal, this would have made her feel quite uncomfortable as it did not conform to her inner image of herself.

With some help on my part, Elizabeth was helped to understand and overcome her problem and thus break the power of the conditioning that had caused her to be a victim for most of her life.

In Elizabeth's case, past-life regression was not necessary as she was able to see quite clearly that the initial cause of all her problems lay in that incident that took place when she was just ten years old. But had looking at earlier periods in her current life not produced any helpful results, I would then have suggested that we go on to look at events in one or more of her previous lives in case that was where the solution to the problem lay.

It is not difficult to see that if a single incident in one person's current life can lead to years of difficulty and negativity, incidents that have been enlarged and repeated over the course of one or more previous lives can give rise to problems that are even more difficult to deal with.

It is possible for each of us, with a little help if necessary, to overcome the effects of such victimization and move on. There is another saying, 'No one can make me a victim without my permission.'

SELF-ESTEEM

If progress through our various lives is to bring with it any sort of personal evolvement, it follows that we should use our experiences to try to improve ourselves and the way in which we live those lives. One thing that greatly affects how we live – whether in present or past lives – is our inner view of ourselves and our own worth – in other words, our self-esteem.

You have already read about the way in which our feelings about ourselves are greatly affected by the actions and attitudes of those with whom we come into contact. Although it is impossible to change the past and the way in which we have been treated, it is quite possible to change the effect that treatment is going to have on the rest of our current life. By changing the remainder of this life for the better, we can allow ourselves to progress further on our multi-lifetime journey so that we are nearer to attaining our final goal than before.

One of the most difficult things for anyone to deal with – and one that affects self-esteem more than almost anything else – is a sense of rejection. This applies even when the perceived rejection was unintentional or unavoidable. A young child whose parent sadly dies experiences the same sense of inner rejection as the one whose father or mother decides to go off and leave the family. Logic does not come into this. Children are not able to reason that the parent may not have wished to go and would have been much happier if he or she had been able to remain. All that children feel is that this person – the one they consider to be wonderful and all-knowing – has gone away and left them behind. In the mind of such children, this means that the parent did not love them enough to stay – and this in turn leads to the belief that they are 'unlovable'.

Naturally, as children grow older and such things are explained to them, they can understand that the death of their parent was not a sign that anyone wanted to leave them or that they were not worthy of love — but the damage has already been done. The deeper subconscious feelings about ourselves are formed at a very early age and common sense alone is not going to change that inner opinion. For changes to take place and for individuals to improve their self-esteem, two steps are necessary:

• Firstly, the person needs to understand just why they have a low opinion of themselves. It could be because of the type of loss already mentioned or perhaps they were constantly compared unfavourably with a sibling. Maybe they were brought up in a family where the members found it very difficult to display their emotions openly and so, because love was never overtly shown, the child believed that it was not forthcoming. There could be any number of different reasons and, with or without help, the former child must learn to recognize them.

• Secondly, they need to be able to change that inner perception of themselves — and this is where hypnotherapy can prove such a valuable aid. Patients can be helped to look deep into their subconscious mind and find the child they once were. By learning to love that inner child unconditionally they can overcome poor self-esteem and lack of confidence in themselves.

REJECTION THROUGH THE LIFETIMES

Just as the adult today can learn to overcome the poor self-esteem caused by feelings of rejection as a child, so people in a current life can learn to deal with the many rejections of former incarnations. In doing so, they can break the pattern so that they do not have to keep re-experiencing those feelings.

This fact seems particularly important when you recall that we continually encounter many of the same people as we journey through our various lives. If one person, in however many roles and guises, has caused you to feel rejected or inferior during several lifetimes, you are likely to experience that feeling instinctively when meeting him or her in the current one. You may not even realize that this is happening but, because it is, you will automatically act towards that person as though you expect him or her to reject you. If you do this, human nature will probably lead that person to do so. Thus the problem is perpetuated.

If you are helped by a sympathetic therapist to recognize what has happened over the course of your previous lives, you can certainly be helped to change your inner perceptions and therefore the way in which you act. You will put an end to what has been an ongoing situation and, because of this, you will take great strides forwards in your own development.

Even those who have sought to find out about their previous lives purely out of curiosity often find that many personal benefits accompany the understanding that this discovery brings about.

INHERITANCE

We do not only inherit characteristics and tendencies from our biological parents, but also from our past 'selves'. As we may have been of any race, creed or colour, we may not necessarily bring with us into this life the physical characteristics of the previous ones but we are often the bearers of talents, emotions and traits. We have all heard of people such as Mozart who were able at a very young age to display a vast talent in their particular field. We may have wondered how it was possible for Mozart to have so much knowledge and ability in the field of music while still only a small child. But, if you entertain the thought that perhaps he was continuing with a skill and ability learned in a previous life (as opposed to beginning again in this one) it does not seem so difficult to understand.

This might also apply to those children who, from time to time, reach such high academic standards that they are able to pass their university entrance examinations at the age of ten or eleven years. Every now and then, we read in the newspapers of a six year old child who was able to beat the world's Grand Masters at chess, or we hear of a five-year-old sinking a hole-in-one on the golf course. These children, too, have probably brought their talents with them from a previous life – although whether you consider this brings them much happiness is another matter.

The experience of many practising regression hypnotherapists shows that, in the majority of cases, when we see what we term 'genius' or 'a child prodigy' in this lifetime, that person actually had their previous life cut short, whether through illness or misadventure. This prevented them from fulfilling their potential at that time and their spirit appears to have chosen to continue on the same path in their current life.

This 'carrying over' from one lifetime to another is not restricted to particular creative talents. Personality traits, behavioural tendencies and emotional states – any or all of these can be 'inherited' from our former selves.

These can be positive or negative characteristics. Once again, it seems that such inheritance is more commonly brought forward when the person's former lifespan was shorter than was normal for their time. It seems as though the spirit, not having been given the opportunity to develop that aspect of the individual fully in one life, feels compelled to carry it forward in order to complete the process.

As we look back through history, it is possible to see that genius rarely seems to be accompanied by happiness. Many who have had exceptional creative talents lived lives that were tormented by their mental or emotional state – indeed several artistic and musical geniuses resorted to taking their own lives as the only means of escape. This pattern does not have to persist – and possibly the reason for the spirit to choose to re-experience the genius state is to prove that this is so.

It is up to those individuals who are the possessors of exceptional ability (or perhaps to those around them) to ensure that they lead as balanced a life as possible. Of course, those who have a particular talent are likely to want to develop it and should be given the opportunity to do so. But it is also essential that they find time for other aspects of life so that they may become more rounded and therefore more contented people.

This is another area that indicates the value of experiencing past lives through regression. Sometimes it is only by looking back at what has gone before that we acquire the knowledge and desire to change what is to come.

AFTER THE REGRESSION
It is not only the actual session of past-life regression that is important or that provides information. That is simply a case of 'opening the door'. Further facts often come to mind in the weeks following the session itself.

Although many people, particularly those who are on a path of inner discovery, wish to have a number of past-life regression sessions, they are usually advised to leave an interval of six to eight weeks between each one. This is because new information often makes itself apparent for some time after each experience of past-life regression.

Sometimes new knowledge comes to the person in the form of a dream. This is probably one instance where it is most difficult to distinguish between actual information and figments of the imagination. But, while outsiders may say that the whole thing is pure imagination, those who have experienced it seem to be able to tell the difference between the dream state and the acquiring of further information.

One woman told her therapist that there were times when, although she did not wake, she 'knew' on some inner level that she was asleep and that what she was seeing in her mind was not just a dream but an extension of what she had experienced during her session of past-life regression. Unfortunately such 'knowledge' is impossible to prove – but it is usually quite clear to those who experience it.

Another way in which the woman concerned was able to distinguish between information and a dream was that, having been dreaming, as soon as she awoke the dream seemed to disappear and she could remember very little of it. When she had been given more facts about a previous life, however, she was able to recall every detail after she woke.

There is also waking knowledge. Sometimes this can occur spontaneously. The person may be having a meal, walking down the street or even relaxing in a chair when – as if from nowhere – further facts about a past life suddenly present themselves. In many cases, these facts are fine details that fill in the gaps that occurred during the regression session itself.

For example, because direct, closed questions are difficult to answer when being regressed, detailed responses may well occur after the event. One man – who had been a woman in the former life he had experienced – was walking round a department store when he suddenly found himself able to give the names of his three children in that earlier life – something he had been unable to do when asked the direct question by the hypnotherapist at the time.

The man had not been trying to remember those names; in fact, he was not thinking about the regression at all as he wandered around that store. In a way, the names were irrelevant as they made no difference to what he had experienced of that former life. Nevertheless, he was absolutely convinced that the names that had come to him were correct.

MEDITATION

People who are used to meditating often find that this is the ideal way of increasing their knowledge about a former life. As they are able to relax deeply when they meditate, they put up no barriers to whatever information presents itself. Whether using this method or any other, it is important not to try to force the information to come. For one thing, such effort of will reduces the level of relaxation considerably. For another, you are less likely to believe whatever knowledge you receive as you will always wonder whether you have simply imagined it.

The most effective method is to start meditating, using whichever technique you would normally use, and then begin thinking about what you already know about your past life. See it in your mind, almost as though you were watching a home movie or a video, and just let it go on playing. You will find that your mind takes over and gives you details you did not even know you were seeking but that once you have them, you are positive are correct.

It is at such times of increased awareness that the lessons of one or more of your previous lives may become apparent to you. Just as it is often easier for the outsider to see the root cause of a problem, you may find that being fully relaxed or even thinking of other things may put you at sufficient distance from the past life to enable you to understand what you were supposed to have learned from it.

[VIII]

LONG-TERM EFFECTS

There are times, although they are not frequent, when the physical signs of something that happened during a session of past-life regression show themselves, either during the regression itself or immediately afterwards. At other times it is interesting to note the link between permanent marks that subjects have now and events that occurred to them in their previous lives.

Therapists have known for a long time that a strong link exists between mind and body. We all know how, if we are anxious, our breathing becomes shallow, the heart and pulse race and we think less clearly. Similarly, extreme tension can lead to many conditions including migraine, constipation, PMT and aching muscles.

The converse can also be true in that our physical health may well influence our mental state. The person who is suffering serious ill health is naturally likely to feel somewhat depressed while the one who is taking a combination of prescribed medications may, owing to their side effects, end up feeling either morose or 'high'.

People with long-term physical conditions may learn to block out pain, using whatever technique their mind has created for them. One woman taught herself to think of her pain as a 'different feeling', rather than one that hurt her. A man in hospital awaiting a gallbladder operation used to 'hang his pain on a hook on the wall of the ward'. This meant he was able to talk to his wife and children without needing to be under the influence of painkilling medication that made it difficult for him to think or speak clearly.

PHYSICAL REACTIONS DURING A REGRESSION SESSION

Some people – usually those who are most able to relax deeply when hypnotic trance is induced – show clear physical reactions to the circumstances in which they find themselves during a past life experience. If they find themselves in a very cold place, goose pimples may appear on the surface of their skin. On the other hand, should they be somewhere extremely hot, they may begin to perspire. This is not unpleasant for them – indeed, in most cases they are not even aware that it is happening.

At other times the reactions will occur after the regression is over. Again, there is no pain or discomfort to accompany the physical signs and they usually fade within ten to twenty minutes.

Adrian

Adrian was regressed to a life in Ancient Egypt where he said he was a young woman living at home with her fairly well-to-do family. At some point this woman witnessed a murder taking place and, having been seen by the murderer, was captured and taken from her home.

The murderer obviously decided that it was necessary to silence this witness permanently and this was done in a horrific way. She was dragged into a room in which there was a stone chest. When the lid was lifted she was able to see that the chest contained several writhing venomous snakes. The murderer forced the woman to plunge her arm into the centre of this mass and she received several poisonous bites, from which she subsequently died.

It must be pointed out here that, because the detachment technique was used throughout, at no point did Adrian experience physical discomfort or fear. He merely reported what he was seeing as if watching a film. It is also interesting to note that at no time prior to the regression, during it, or at any time afterwards, has Adrian suffered from a phobia about snakes.

What did happen, however, was that, when the regression was over, Adrian found that he had on his arm several pairs of red dots – as if he had indeed received a number of snake bites. Those marks did not hurt – they did not even irritate – and they disappeared completely after about ten minutes.

CURRENT BODY MARKS

At other times, events revealed during the regression tally with marks the subjects currently carry on their body. For example, a young man who, in his past life, received a fatal gunshot wound in the United States during the gangster era, currently has a birthmark on his back in exactly the same place where the bullet entered his body.

Of course, it is difficult in such cases to be certain whether there is a direct link between the injury and the birthmark or whether, having been shot in his past life, the young man had somehow caused the bullet to enter his body at a place where he already had a mark.

What is certain, however, is that, whichever is the case, it serves to reinforce the strong link between mind and body.

GUILT

Whether we are thinking about this life or a previous one, guilt can cause many reactions over which we appear to have no control. But, because guilt plays such a major part in so many people's lives, it is something we all have to learn to deal with and one of those lessons with which the spirit is confronted on its journey through the lifetimes.

Guilt is a useless emotion unless it enables us to learn something. There is a difference, of course, between the guilt we experience when we have done something wrong by accident and that resulting from intentional wrongdoing. In the former case, the best we can is do is apologize and try to put the matter right. If it is not possible to atone in a way that directly corresponds to the original fault, perhaps we can do some other type of good deed to show our regret.

However, if someone has deliberately set out to harm another person or commit a crime, then, as well as trying to make amends, it is necessary to learn from what was done and to make an active decision never to repeat former errors. Once we have done our best to deal with the problems caused by the wrongdoing in whatever way was thought appropriate, it is necessary to let the guilt go if it is not to influence and affect the rest of our life. Guilt for something done in the past, even when it is sincerely regretted and everything possible has been done to put matters right, is responsible for many instances of mental, emotional and even physical ill-health.

If people are capable of damaging their current lives because of guilt about former misdeeds, this is also true about wrongdoings committed in one or more of their former lives. However, there are a few points to bear in mind:

- Any person living today has been guilty of some sort of wrongdoing or inadequacy in a former life. Once we reach the stage where we behave perfectly in all circumstances, we do not need to come back and live another life on earth.

- If that wrongdoing was atoned for during the former life, we should be able to release ourselves from the guilt and go forward in this one. We may, of course, do other things that we regret during the current life but, if the spirit is to progress, lessons once learned can be set aside so that we can go on and cope with the things we have to learn in the present.

- In some cases it is necessary to look closely at the original incident that caused the ensuing guilt. Was it something we truly did wrong or was it something that was wrong only for the time in which we were living but that would be treated with more compassion today? There was a time when men and women were deported for stealing loaves of bread to feed their starving families; they would not be treated so harshly today.

The opposite also holds true. Terrible crimes were committed in the past that at the time were seen as right and just by the perpetrators. No reasonable person today would condone torture chambers, slavery or enforced child labour – yet those things were at one time considered 'normal' and 'acceptable'. If, during the course of a regression session, you discover that you were involved in something that is now abhorrent to you but which at that time would have seemed right and proper, there is no value in carrying that guilt with you throughout this life. The very fact that you now find the deed abhorrent means that you have learned from what you did and so you should feel free to let the guilt go.

Sometimes the guilt that is felt is not justified at all but is created in the mind of the sufferer by the words or actions of someone else. In some cases, minor misdeeds are continually commented upon so that the one who has committed them is made to feel guilty and inferior, whereas in reality the fault lies with the person making the comments. 'You would do it if you loved me' is a form of emotional blackmail that has been used for generations to induce in the victim a sense of guilt and therefore a compliance with the wishes of the blackmailer.

There have been times when understanding the past reason that underlies a current inner sense of guilt has released a sufferer from a debilitating physical condition in the present life. One woman – a gentle and non-violent person today – was regressed to a time when she was a warder in the debtors' prison at Newgate. In that life she was avaricious and cruel and would silence noisy or troublesome prisoners by beating them about the head with a huge cudgel. In this life she continually suffered from excruciating migraines for no apparent reason.

Although she was full of contempt for the person she had been in that former life, I was able to work with that woman to help her understand that she – the person she is now, was not responsible in any way for her former self's actions, and the fact that she was now such a different personality indicated that she had learned the necessary lesson and could therefore release herself from the guilt that she had been carrying. From that time her migraines vanished, never to reappear.

THE LAW OF KARMA

Those who accept the existence of the Law of Karma see it as a form of cosmic retribution for past sins. This ensures that we reap the consequences of our past actions – whether the deeds were committed in this life or in a previous one. Most religions in both the Eastern and Western world believe in a form of karma – although they may not call it by that name. Whether one talks of 'an eye for an eye and a tooth for a tooth' (which is wrongly interpreted by some as meaning that it is permissible to exact personal revenge) or whether one believes that, with no assistance from us, the wrongdoer will be punished, the concept of retribution is accepted.

'WHY ME?'

There are times when each of us may ask the question, 'Why me?' when some hardship strikes or tragedy befalls us. A belief in karma helps some people to deal with the emotions aroused by this question. And a belief in reincarnation can give further explanation, although it does not of itself remove the pain or distress experienced by the questioner. We have all heard of cases where a truly good person, who has never done deliberate harm to another, suffers a dreadful and terrifying illness. Similarly, there are cases of very young children who not even having lived long enough to know what harm means, lose their lives. On such occasions it is not unusual to hear someone ask how, if there is a God, such things can be allowed to happen. Perhaps the answer is to be found in reincarnation and that the current suffering is some sort of retribution for wrongs committed in a former life.

No one can prove whether this is so or not, but for some people it helps to provide an answer to the eternal question, 'Why me?'

The Law of Karma removes the necessity for anyone to exact personal vengeance upon another – which is not the same as saying that there should be no justice. If you believe that all is just 'fate' and that there is no such thing as a God or a higher power, then personal vengeance achieves nothing other than bringing you down to the level of the person on whom you have revenged yourself.

If you believe that karma exists, there is no need for you to take personal revenge as this ancient law ensures that the person concerned gets his or her just desserts – whether in this life or in another. If karma does exist, the way in which it shows itself is not always obvious. We all know that if we misuse a machine it will eventually break down and refuse to serve us. In the same way, if we misuse our bodies – perhaps by smoking excessively, being inactive or over-indulgent – it is likely that we will suffer some form of ill-health as a result. But karma goes far deeper than that.

In the north of London lives a woman whose son is seriously handicapped, both mentally and physically. This woman – I'll call her Sheila – has an extremely difficult life. Her husband left her when their son was a baby and she spends her whole time every day caring for this boy, who can do almost nothing for himself.

It would be easy for an outsider to look at the boy and wonder whether he had done some terrible thing in a previous life and is perhaps being punished in this one. But the boy himself is quite happy in his own way. He does not understand the nature of his condition or how different he is from other children. The one who is really suffering is his mother. Although she loves her son dearly and is willing to do all she can for him, she finds the process distressing, exhausting and frightening as she contemplates a time when she may not be around to look after him. If there is karma, perhaps it is the mother who is being asked to pay.

If you feel that some misfortune in your life may be caused by karmic retribution for something you have done wrong in a previous life, this does not mean that you should give up all hope of ever being happy again. Perhaps you are being given a taste of this misfortune in order to overcome it and learn to live a contented life, even if not in the way you had originally intended.

Consider two people who, as the result of tragic accidents, are seriously injured and find themselves confined thereafter to life in a wheelchair. One may accept his fate and spend the rest of his life mourning his disability and pining for what might have been. The other may go on to develop those of his muscles that do function and become a disabled sportsman – or may use his brain to find ways of helping others in the same position as himself. In this way karma can be part of a positive learning experience.

THE POWER OF THE MIND

The human mind is amazingly powerful and affects our lives in more ways than many of us realize. The condition of our health, our physical capabilities as well as the events we attract and the successes we achieve – all these are directly affected by our positive or negative attitude of mind.

From the young mother who lifts the front wheels of her car in order to release her trapped toddler, to the ten year old girl who imagined the 'good soldiers beating the bad soldiers' to overcome the leukaemia from which she suffered, there are many documented cases of people achieving the seemingly unachievable by using the power of their own mind.

Those are, of course, positive examples of using one's mind – but there are negative examples too. The extreme pessimist, the person who foresees disaster at every turn, can actually make these things happen simply because he expects them to.

When we talk of the power of the mind, we are really referring to the subconscious mind as this is the source of all our inherent tendencies and instinctive actions. Should there ever be a conflict between the conscious and the subconscious mind, the subconscious wins on every occasion. So, however much we decide that we are going to succeed at something, it will not necessarily happen if we fail to harness the power of the subconscious.

Take a simple example – two people sitting an examination. Everyone feels a little nervous before such an event – and this is not altogether a bad thing as this nervousness helps the adrenaline to flow which, provided it is not excessive, induces quicker, clearer thought. But, assuming that each student has revised thoroughly for the exam, it is those who keep telling themselves how nervous they are and that they are bound to fail who are likely to do so. The ones who have deliberately harnessed the power of their subconscious mind so that they see themselves working calmly through the paper and succeeding at the end of it are the ones who will achieve their aim.

VISUALIZATION

The way to channel the power of the subconscious mind is by the use of visualization. This means nothing more than seeing pictures in your mind and ensuring that those pictures show the positive outcome you desire. This process needs to be repeated several times over a given period.

The subconscious mind is unable to tell the difference between what is real and what is imagined, so it accepts each imagined success as a real one. In other words, a positive student's subconscious accepts that she has passed an exam every day for as long as she has been visualizing. When the date of the actual test comes along, this provides the student with the confidence of a person who really has done what she has been imagining.

PSYCHOSOMATIC ILLNESS

Misuse of the power of the mind can cause emotional problems and even psychosomatic illness. People who are convinced that they are a failure or don't deserve to succeed will, indeed, fail. Those whose mind convinces them that every small twinge is a sign of some terrible illness that is creeping up on them are quite likely to develop that illness.

Hypnotherapy, often combined with the use of past-life regression, can help negative individuals to understand and eventually reverse that negativity so that they begin to harness the power of their subconscious mind in a positive way leading to success in life, whatever that term may mean to them.

MIND POWER AND SPORT

Look into the face of a champion sportsman or woman immediately before an event. As well as the necessary concentration, there is an expression that shows that, even before the starter's gun has sounded, they have 'seen' themselves performing brilliantly. It is no coincidence that sports people all over the world – teams as well as individuals – are now employing sports psychologists to help them achieve this.

PAST LIVES AND THE POWER OF THE MIND

Knowledge and experience of your former lives can help you to uncover any negativity you might have brought with you to the current life and this, in turn, enables you to go forward and eliminate that negativity so that you turn this current life into the positive experience you would wish it to be.

For those who have on-going problems in today's life, great benefit may sometimes be derived from exploring one or more of their former lives. This applies particularly to those people whose problems are emotional or psychological. However, help can also be found when seeking to overcome physical ailments.

The problem that benefits most often from the exploration of one or more past lives is probably that of phobia. Phobias are among the conditions most often and most effectively treated by means of hypnotherapy. Provided the patient co-operates fully with the hypnotherapist, a cure is almost guaranteed.

In some instances, it is possible to treat a phobia sufferer successfully without discovering the initial cause of the problem – but the patient usually derives great benefit from identifying what that cause was. A phobia is by definition an 'illogical fear', so sufferers often feel foolish or inadequate for being frightened of something that does not bother other people at all. Discovering the root cause of the fear removes that sense of inferiority as a reason for their reaction has been revealed and so the fear is now no longer 'illogical'.

In most cases the hypnotherapist will, with their patients' co-operation, begin by exploring earlier events in their current life to see if the cause of the phobia can be found. If this is unsuccessful, they will then go on to look into one or more of their former lives. When this is done it is very rare indeed to find no basis for the phobia.

Some people claim that patients exploring a past life in this way simply 'invent' a reason for the current phobia. In a very few cases that could perhaps be true – although in the majority of cases it is possible by later research to confirm that it is not. But, even if the cause of the phobia was an invention of the patient's subconscious mind, does it really matter? If it enables someone to go forward and live a life free of a phobia that has been crippling him or her emotionally and affecting every day of that life, whether the 'memory' was real or imagined is irrelevant.

Finding the initial cause of a phobia does not cure it instantaneously. It is still necessary for the hypnotherapist to work with the patient to overcome the results of whatever it was that happened in the past – although this will probably take no more than two or three sessions. But, if the cause has not been found, nothing will be done to eliminate the patient's sense of inferiority for having suffered from the phobia in the first place.

simon

Simon suffered from claustrophobia – but with a difference. Whereas, for most claustrophobics, the fear is of being shut in an enclosed space, Simon had no fear of lifts, aeroplanes, small rooms, and so on – unless there were several other people shut in with him. His claustrophobia arose when he was indoors, even in a large place such as a supermarket or a department store, only if the place was crowded. In the manner of many phobics, he would begin to panic, his heart would race, his breathing would become shallow and he would feel as though he was about to faint.

Simon came to me seeking help in overcoming his problem. Analysis of his youth and childhood did not reveal any reason for his fears. In fact, when regressed to the time in his current life when he was a baby, Simon experienced the same sense of panic when in a room with several other people present. He was regressed to a former life, when, Simon said, he was a young man living in southern Spain about a century ago.

He and his friends were attending a fiesta on a feast day and the atmosphere was bright and convivial. There were crowds of people in the square of the small town but, even though he was surrounded, he had no sense of fear at all. Then, perhaps because of the excitement or perhaps because of the extreme heat, the young man began to feel dizzy. He stumbled and fell to the ground, unnoticed by his friends or by any of the mass of people surrounding him. After that, all he could describe were dozens of feet around him as he was accidentally trampled to death.

When the regression was over, Simon had no difficulty in understanding how his fear of crowded places had developed. Not only had his life ended in such a tragic way but no one had been sufficiently aware of what was happening to be able to help him as he fell to the ground. So what began as a friendly mass of people became his enemy and, eventually, his murderers.

Once he was able to understand the reason for his emotions and realized that he was not an inadequate person for experiencing them, Simon was able to work with me to cure the phobia once and for all.

HEALING PHYSICAL PROBLEMS

Some conditions, particularly asthma, migraine and skin problems such as eczema and psoriasis, often have their origins in a former life. It is well known that these conditions are made worse by mental factors such as stress and physiological problems such as certain foods – and that may be to do with problems in their current life. However, some people also seem to be born with a tendency to these disorders.

Of course it is right that physiological reasons for such conditions should be explored so that sufferers can avoid any irritants that may be uncovered. The asthmatic may be adversely affected by aerosols, some types of pollen or certain perfumes, the migraine sufferer is often advised to avoid chocolate, red wine and cheese, and the person suffering from skin problems may have to choose cosmetics and preparations that are designed specifically for those with skin allergies.

Once all this has be done, however, and once sufferers have been taught how to reduce their stress level, it can be truly beneficial to look to the past to discover whether there is a deeper reason for their condition. Some typical situations that come to mind include:

- The asthmatic who was suffocated in a previous life.
- The migraine sufferer who suffered a severe blow to the head that, although it did not kill him, affected his mental state thereafter.
- The woman suffering from psoriasis who, as a servant in a previous life, had been responsible for preparing poisonous substances to rid his master's house of vermin – and whose hands had been damaged as a result.

As in the case of a phobia, knowledge of how the initial problem arose will not of itself bring about a cure. But, provided patients also follow the advice given to them by their medical practitioner and take advantage of the help offered by their hypnotherapist, they are thereafter able to deal with the problem far more effectively than if the original cause had never been known.

LIFE IN THE WOMB

It is possible, by means of hypnosis, to regress patients to the time when they were a baby in their mother's womb, and there have been occasions when the cause of a later problem was discovered there.

Alison

Alison consulted me because she was suffering from both migraine and claustrophobia and was unable to remember a time in her life when this had not been so. Indeed, her mother told her that, when she was a tiny baby in her pram, she would scream in terror if the rainhood was put up and would sometimes appear to have pains in her head for which no medical reason could be found.

Alison and I decided that it would be advisable to explore her past lives to see if we could discover a reason for her problems and so I began to regress her. However, instead of returning to a former life, Alison's subconscious took her back to her time as an unborn child in her mother's womb.

It will be helpful here to explain a little about the background. Alison's mother had previously suffered three miscarriages because, in each case, she had gone into labour far too soon. To prevent the same problem happening again, when she became pregnant with Alison, the mother had a small operation that involved stitching the neck of the womb until it was time for the baby to be born.

The unborn Alison, wanting to make her entry into the world far too early, found she was unable to escape from this closed-in place and this had induced in her a sense of panic that, after her birth, translated itself into claustrophobia. In addition, in her desperate efforts to escape from the place in which she found herself trapped, the unborn baby, having turned to be in the birth position, had banged her head, time and time again, on the place through which she was eventually able to be born. Hence the migraine.

At the end of the session, Alison was not only able to understand the reasons behind her complaints but she could also see that, had she been able to be born when she wished it, she probably would not have survived.

The regression over, the usual course of action would be two or three sessions of hypnotherapy to enable Alison to overcome her long-term problems but for once this did not prove to be necessary. We did not have to go on to deal with the problems of migraine and claustrophobia in the usual way; the understanding of what had happened to her as an unborn child was sufficient to bring about a cure.

ANGER

Whether directed towards other people or, as in many cases, turned in upon oneself, anger can be the most destructive of emotions. In many instances it is possible to look back over a previous life – or over a series of lives – and see how that anger has built up without ever having been given the opportunity to be released.

There are, of course, occasions when any one of us might justifiably feel angry. To see an obvious injustice – or to be the victim of it oneself – might make you angry. The same might be said of many other wrongs, from meaningless and petty officiousness to the wanton destruction of the earth's resources.

However, for anger to be beneficial it must have an outlet. To be angry but do nothing about the cause of that anger is simply a waste of time. The anger itself only serves a purpose when it acts as a spur and the person who feels angry steps in to prevent an injustice being done, starts a campaign or writes a strongly worded letter. That is using anger as a means towards a positive end.

Consider what happens if that anger is not used. Either it turns inwards to eat away at those who feel it, causing them to become negative and bitter or, having no proper direction in which to go, it is aimed at the first or nearest person to come along. And so we hear of instances of 'road rage', senseless violence, vandalism or rioting.

Anger is an energy and energy needs to be put to use. Think of a pressure cooker within which steam is building up. If there were no outlet for that steam, the result would be an enormous explosion. This is why it is important that, if there is no obvious means of escape for your anger, you need to find some other way of releasing that energy before it does harm to you or to someone else. Go for a fast run, kick a ball, dig a garden – or even punch a cushion, if that is the best thing to hand.

In some ways, anger turned in upon itself is even more dangerous as it can do great harm to the sufferer. Not only will it cause unhappiness, negativity and low self-esteem but, in some cases, physical problems will arise. Complementary therapists and enlightened members of the medical profession now accept that many conditions, including ulcers, insomnia, and even some cases of cancer, can be caused or exacerbated by this build-up of inward-turned anger.

Although injustice and hardship certainly exist at the present time, it was probably even more prevalent in past centuries. Those were often times when the ordinary person was far less able to do anything about unjust situations or even to voice his opinion about unjust events. Rule was stricter, punishment more severe, and freedom of speech far more restricted than today, so it is little wonder that people experienced a far greater accumulation of internalized anger throughout their lives.

This is why exploring a series of past lives can be so beneficial. If you are able to see that in a number of previous incarnations you were placed in a position where it was impossible to release the anger you felt, you can understand how it is that you may have been born into your present life with an accumulation of anger already within you.

This discovery does not in itself provide a cure – but it is a vital stepping-stone. The same therapist who helps you to examine those past lives and the information and emotions you have collected along the way can also help you to deal with today's anger and learn to find a positive outlet for what is a potentially destructive energy.

Many of those who have found a means of harnessing the energy of anger have gone on to make real and valuable changes to the world. The authors who were the 'angry young men' of the 1960s, campaigners on behalf of the environment, those who were made angry by the sight of abandoned orphans in Romania, and those who are unable to tolerate the cruel treatment of animals in certain countries, all these people have used their anger as a positive force for good, thereby helping the world and, at the same time, taking giant steps in their own personal evolvement.

fEAR

Just like anger, fear is a destructive emotion capable of doing great harm to the sufferer and to those with whom he or she comes into frequent contact. A frightened person will usually go one of two ways: they will either retreat into themselves, thereby living a miserable existence, or they will hit out at others in order to prevent them from doing it first.

The person who is constantly fearful has a sad existence. Even when nothing is going wrong, they are waiting for something terrible to happen. He or she may even avoid taking a full part in life, instead remaining on the outer perimeter for fear of befalling some unknown calamity.

Negativity attracts more negativity, so the fearful person often attracts the type of behaviour from others that only serves to increase that fearfulness. Think of those children who start school feeling terrified of the other children. Unfortunately, bullies seem to have an unerring instinct for recognizing this fear and picking on people who suffer from it. The treatment they receive simply convinces the frightened ones that they were right to have this sense of fear in the first place.

Fear can also turn frightened people into bullies themselves, making them believe that, if they strike out first, no one will torment them. This may be true but such behaviour does nothing to break the cycle of fear, either for the individuals concerned or the community at large.

As in the case of anger, we can learn a great deal about ourselves, the fear we suffer and the reasons for it, by examining several of our past lives. Once again we can see how there were so many more things to be afraid of in previous times – and far less we could do about situations that arose.

The slave frightened of the ruler may have had good reason for his fear if there was a danger of losing his life at the whim of his master, should he fail to obey all commands instantly. The sailor fearing for his life during a storm on the high seas had a poorer likelihood of survival than his modern counterparts. When both corporal and capital punishment were commonplace world-wide, many minor offenders had cause to experience fear.

Even though those same situations may no longer exist in most parts of the civilized world, it is possible to examine one person's series of previous lives and see how the fear was real for him or her through lifetime after lifetime until it reached its current level. The situation is made even worse when you consider that fear does not remain static. Like many other negative emotions, if nothing is done to help sufferers free themselves from the fear and anxiety they experience, it will grow worse until they receive help.

Past-life regression is one of the most beneficial ways of helping to remove a constant sense of fear. The hypnotherapist assists the patient to examine several different past lives. These will not necessarily be experienced in chronological order but it will be left to the patient's subconscious mind to select the most appropriate incarnation to examine at each regression session. The reason for this is that the most recent life may perhaps have been so traumatic that the patient would not yet be able to cope with what is revealed. Once subjects have grown used to the technique and to the fact that they are not going to feel any pain or distress during the session, they are far more likely to want to probe even more of their previous lives.

After that, it is rather like peeling the layers of outer skin from an onion until the firm, crisp and healthy portion inside is revealed. As the fears caused by each life are examined, discussed and understood, the weight appears to lift from patients until the time comes when they are able to move positively throughout their current life again.

Naturally, a certain amount of logical fear is a good thing as it encourages caution. No one wants to be so foolhardy that they plunge their hand into the flames of a fire or take unnecessary risks in some other way. Natural fear is a protector, whether we are talking about physical action or emotional involvement. But if the suit of armour is too thick it is impossible to breathe.

Without taking calculated risks there is no sense of achievement in life. The natural fear experienced should be put to good purpose so that those concerned do all they can to ensure essential safety precautions are taken. But to put an end to crippling fear is to take another step on your path of evolvement and to learn a lesson during this lifetime so that you never have to be faced with it again.

DEPRESSION

Depression is one of the most debilitating of conditions, frequently causing sufferers to feel that they have no means of escape. While medication may suppress some of the symptoms, it does nothing to remove the basic causes of the condition. (It should be emphasized here that what is being referred to is not manic depression, which has a physiological cause, but the type of depression that is brought about by a sense of hopelessness and a feeling of low self-esteem.)

One of the most frustrating aspects of depression for those who suffer from it is the sense that there is no escape. In many cases the original reason for the condition cannot be recalled so that there appears to be no way to deal with it. In addition, depressives often feel that there is no cure available to them. If they take antidepressants to relieve the symptoms, they are in danger of becoming addicted to them and, in any event, as soon as they try to stop or cut down the number they take, those symptoms often return to torment them again.

Hypnotherapy, psychotherapy or counselling can be of benefit when the original cause of the depression is known but many patients feel that, without this knowledge, they have no hope of escaping from the vicious circle in which they are trapped. This is where past-life regression as a therapy can come into its own.

Depression often arises from a sense of hopelessness and a feeling of inadequacy because of an inability to take charge of one's own life. In many instances, looking back into past incarnations can show how this may have been the case one or more lifetimes ago and how patients have brought those feelings with them into their current life.

We are now encouraged to take charge of our life and to 'stand on our own two feet', but there was a time when this would have been impossible, either because of the circumstances that existed during the period or because to have dared to question authority would have led to punishment.

jessica

Jessica had suffered from depression for most of her adult life. She had been prescribed antidepressants by her doctor but found that these made her feel lethargic and uncomfortable, so she decided to seek another method of help. She came to see me and, having discussed the events of her current life with her, I suggested that we try examining her past lives. Having reached the stage where she was willing to try almost anything, Jessica agreed.

The first two sessions of past-life regression did not disclose anything that was likely to have caused her current condition. There had been various problems in these lives – as in any – but none that directly related to the depression she now experienced.

On the third occasion, Jessica spoke of a hard life she had lived as a 'below stairs' servant called Martha working in the home of a well-to-do family in London at the beginning of the twentieth century. Coming from a very poor family, Martha had gone into service at the age of eleven and, from that time, had seen her parents and brother on very few occasions. Being the youngest of the servants employed in the house, Martha was given the most menial of tasks, working very long hours and sharing a cold attic bedroom with three other girls. She had no contact at all with the family who employed her but was given her instructions by other, more senior, members of staff.

It is easy to understand how such a situation must have been really distressing for someone who was no more than a child. As Martha told her story she said that the worst thing of all was that she could see no end to it. The most she could hope for in the coming years was to rise a little in the hierarchy of the household – but this still meant years of hard work, long hours and poor conditions. At the same time, she knew she did not dare to complain about her lot because, as was frequently pointed out to her, there were far more young girls seeking work than there were positions for them.

In her seventeenth year, Martha became ill, the years of hard toil and poor conditions having taken their toll. No one was inclined to call the doctor for a lowly servant girl and, a few months later, Martha died.

This was Jessica's last incarnation before her current one and, after we had looked at it and discussed it together, it was easy to understand how, having been given no help or comfort during that miserable existence, she had brought with her to her present life the same feelings of hopelessness and despair. She was then able to co-operate with me as we worked together to put the distant past behind her and deal successfully with her current symptoms.

[IX]

RELATIONSHIPS

Everyone has relationship problems from time to time. Most of these problems are dealt with satisfactorily or are resolved by the passage of time. Sometimes, however, relationship problems are either incapable of resolution or people find themselves in the same situation – albeit with different people – time after time.

SPIRIT CHOICES
When the spirit is about to enter a new life, not only does it choose the lessons it is to learn this time (provided those lessons with which it was previously presented have been successfully learned) but it selects the people to whom it is to be born – those who will put it in a position from which it is able to confront those lessons. A certain amount of comfort might be drawn from this knowledge as it means that each of us is on the path of evolvement we have selected, however difficult that path might prove to be.

Indeed, the more difficult the journey through this life, the greater the strides we are making on our spiritual path and the more evolved we have become already. There is a saying, taken from an Eastern philosophy, that 'No man is asked to bear more than he is able to bear'. This also refers to the fact that we are deemed strong enough to cope with whatever may confront us.

ILLOGICAL DISLIKE
One common problem arising from relationship difficulties brought with us from a previous life is an instinctive and seemingly illogical dislike of a particular person – or even of a whole nation of people. There are some people who will tell you that they do not like anyone coming from a particular country – even though they may never have been there or indeed encountered any of its inhabitants. Reason tells us that every nation is made up of good, bad and indifferent people, some of whom we can relate to and others to whom we might not.

Most people are unable to explain these feelings of antipathy. In many such cases it is possible to discover by past-life regression that these people either suffered at the hands of someone from that country or came to great harm while living there. When this is the case, the person concerned can go on to be helped to leave these memories in the past where they belong and to live the rest of their current life free from their illogical prejudices.

There may be several reasons why someone takes an instinctive dislike to a particular individual. It could be that in a past life they suffered harm at the hands of that person or were treated cruelly by him or her. But, in many cases, the reverse is true. If someone has actually been the perpetrator of harm – as opposed to the victim – but has gone on to evolve through the incarnations, it is possible that a strong sense of guilt can cause them to feel extremely uncomfortable when confronted by the one they hurt.

REPEATED RELATIONSHIP DIFFICULTIES

Sometimes a relationship between two people has been so complex throughout several lifetimes that it remains unresolved today. If those two appear to have taken it in turn to harm each other – whether physically, emotionally or mentally – there may well be unresolved business to be completed before they can settle down and either have a harmonious relationship or be content to part company and have no further dealings with each other.

These relationships may not always be played out throughout the lifetimes with the people in the same roles. It could be a mother/child relationship in one lifetime, a husband/wife in another and a servant/master in a third.

Those who have never been regressed often find it very difficult to understand how it is possible to recognize someone from a former life when their outward appearance may be totally different. The only way you can truly understand how this happens is to experience past-life regression for yourself and discover how that knowledge and recognition go far deeper than the surface features.

This recognition – in conjunction with how good or bad the relationship was in one or more former lives – also helps to explain how we may prefer one parent, child or sibling to another, even when each one appears to treat us in the same way. Most mothers, even if they feel guilty about admitting it, will know that, although they may love all their children, they feel particularly close to one of them for no obvious reason they can think of. Well, there is a reason and it is often to be found in a very close relationship in a previous life.

RELATIONSHIP COUNSELLING

Some hypnotherapists use past-life regression as a method of counselling individuals who are experiencing difficulties in their present relationship. This can apply to all relationships, not only those between couples. Each of the people concerned will be regressed individually. Afterwards, they will be able to discuss with the therapist what they have learned from any past knowledge they may have gained about the other person and the feelings created by that person's treatment of them in a previous life.

One of the great benefits of such counselling based on past life experiences is that it removes the necessity for either party to blame the other for what is currently happening. After all, it may be that the cause of all their difficulties came about because of what happened many lifetimes ago.

A SENSE OF INFERIORITY

One might think that a baby could never be born with a sense of inferiority but that something has to happen to that baby as he or she grows in order to instil that feeling. In many cases this is true and it is possible to discover the cause of this inferiority feeling by examining the earlier stages of the patient's current life. But suppose all this examination and probing reveals nothing to which the sense of inferiority could be attributable – in fact the child might even appear to have suffered from it from the time of birth. It is in cases such as this that the exploration of one or more of the patient's former lives can prove helpful.

A DESTRUCTIVE EMOTION

A feeling of inferiority is not only self-perpetuating but actually intensifies with the passing of time. Consider the cycle. You feel that you are less worthy, less able or less loveable than other people and this makes you act as though this feeling was an actual fact. If someone acts like an inferior being, other people will soon treat them as though they are inferior without even stopping to consider the reality of the situation.

In the same instinctive way that a dog can sense a person who is afraid of him, or the mugger can pick out a likely target, or the bully can select his victim, people seem to realize on some subconscious level that certain individuals believe themselves to be inferior. And so the situation is perpetuated.

The only way to put an end to this negative cycle is to discover what it was that caused that sense of inferiority in the first place and to put whatever it was into perspective in the context of the patient's present existence. Assuming that no cause can be uncovered in the current life, past lives should be explored.

FEELING IS NOT NECESSARILY FACT

First thoughts might be that someone who has developed a sense of inferiority may have spent his or her former life in a lowly and submissive position – but this is not always the case. If other people treated you badly then, however elevated your social standing may have been, it is quite possible that you developed such negative feelings about yourself.

One man, in his past life, was the eldest son — and therefore the heir — in an aristocratic French family. However, he was a gentle boy, who was not interested in blood sports or in the military upbringing of other members of the family. His father, feeling that such attitudes were effeminate and brought shame upon the family name, was continually belittling his son, showing him contempt, comparing him unfavourably with his siblings, and mocking him at every opportunity.

Naturally, as would be the case in this lifetime as in any other, the rest of the family copied the attitude of the father. This was partly because they did not wish to incur his displeasure but also partly because such attitudes are contagious, especially when the person being treated in this way does not have the desire or courage to retaliate.

This poor young man grew up hearing nothing but contemptuous comments all around him. Worse still, because of a centuries-old tradition in the family, he was compelled to attend military academy where he was desperately unhappy and where he soon received unfavourable treatment from his superiors as well as from the other cadets.

There is tremendous power in the spoken word. It is a fact that, if someone hears around them nothing but unfavourable comments, they will soon come to accept those comments as the truth. Logic flies out of the window and the victim does not think, 'These people are wrong; I am not inferior to them but simply different.' He begins to believe that what they say must be true.

Words that are constantly repeated have a very strong effect upon the people at whom they are directed. If this were not the case, advertisers would not spend such vast amounts of money repeating their promises and their slogans in order to persuade us to buy their products.

One intelligent and educated woman whose husband had for many years told her that she was 'stupid' said, after the end of the marriage, 'I know I am not stupid but, if you hear something often enough over a long period, you really come to believe it.'

The man who had been miserably treated by his military family in a former life was able, after the regression, to understand why his sense of inferiority had grown to such an extent in that lifetime. If coping with such a situation was the lesson his spirit had chosen to learn in that incarnation, the young man had unfortunately lacked the courage to confront those who verbally tormented him and so the lesson had not been learned. He had therefore brought it with him to his current life so that he might try again. This time, however, the outcome was successful.

POSITIVE GIFTS

We have seen how past-life regression can help to overcome negative beliefs and attitudes brought with us from our previous lives but this should not be taken as an indication that only problems accompany us as we enter our current incarnation. There are many positive outcomes from the lives we have led in the past.

Have you ever wondered why it is that one person has an artistic eye and a flair for colour that appears to be missing from the make-up of the rest of the family? How is it that one child might be able to pick up almost any musical instrument and coax a melody from it while a sibling is tone-deaf and cannot sing a note in tune? You may have noticed how one little girl appears to have an instinctive conception of how mechanical things work while her brothers and sisters struggle just to wire a plug?

It would appear that, if you were expert at some particular skill in a former life, you bring with you to the current one an aptitude for that skill. The carpenter in a previous life might not go on to practise the same trade today – but, whatever his or her job, he would probably be very good at wood-turning or do-it-yourself. The eighteenth-century farmer might work in the city today – but might enjoy gardening as a hobby. And the young mother who does not appear to suffer the same anxieties as many others when it comes to caring for her baby might have been a nanny in an earlier life.

Suppose one of your previous lives was lived in another country, it could be that you either have a feeling of being 'at home' when you visit that country or you find it easier than others to pick up the language.

LESSONS LEARNED

We have already looked at the fact that we have lessons to learn during each incarnation. Sometimes this leads to success and sometimes failure. Although the spirit may have selected those lessons in the first place, it is the human being who either manages to learn them or does not. From some of the examples we have looked at, it is apparent that, if a lesson has not been adequately learned (for whatever reason), the next time that spirit enters a human body it is faced with the same lesson again.

Think of our many lives on this earth as the school that the spirit has to attend. When the work of one class has been successfully completed, the pupil is free to pass on to the next one. If it fails the end-of-term exam, however, it may have to be kept down for a year (or a life) to repeat the same lessons. But, once it passes on to the higher class, it never has to return to the lower one to face those particular challenges again.

We are all faced with innumerable problems during our present lives but we should be able to draw comfort from the fact that, once we have dealt with these problems satisfactorily and have learned from them, we have not only improved our current lives but have taken a giant step on our own evolutionary journey.

It is never too late in life to learn your chosen lessons. If you can look back at your current life and see that the same situation has occurred time after time, let this be the moment at which you decide to do something about it. It may be something you can work out for yourself or you may feel that you need professional help in doing so – the important thing is to overcome any problem so that you never have to be faced with it again.

There are many facets that go to make up the person you are today. Your genes may account for your physical appearance – although, of course, it was your spirit that selected the parents from whom you inherited those genes. Your personality has been formed by the family into which you have been born, and possibly by the astrological positions of the planets at the time of your birth, the events that have surrounded you as you grew and developed – and also by the successes and failures you experienced during your former lives.

'OLD SOULS'

We all know of people, even quite young children, who always seem to be wise beyond their years. These are people who have always been able to cope calmly with most situations and seem instinctively to be able to help and advise others and come up with sensible solutions to various problems. These people are often known as 'old souls' – meaning that it is obvious that their natural wisdom has been acquired from experiences in the lives they have lived in the past.

Some very young children have a particular talent that obviously goes far beyond anything they can have learned in the few years they have spent on earth in their current lifetime. A musical prodigy who not only performed but also composed at a very young age, could not possibly have acquired his talent and knowledge in that small number of years. However, if he had been a talented musician in a former life – and particularly if he died young in that lifetime too – it is quite possible that he was born again already possessing his exceptional musical genius.

From time to time, it is possible to read of very young children who have developed a mathematical or scientific skill far beyond that expected of someone of their age. Some of them even enter university at an age when most others have only just begun their secondary education. Whether this is a good thing or not from the point of view of the child's wellbeing and social life is debatable but the fact that they are able to develop their skills to such an extent while still so young would seem to indicate that they have brought with them into this life the abilities acquired during a former one.

The same applies to those who demonstrate great talent for a particular sport while still extremely young. Of course, these talents, once recognized, are often developed and polished by experts so that the young people achieve very high standards at a very young age. Nonetheless, all the training in the world would not be able to achieve such dramatic results if the natural abilities of the child were not so extraordinary.

Such academic and sporting prowess may be exceptional but it is an unfortunate fact that children who are pushed into performances far beyond those normally associated with their years often go on to lead quite unhappy lives. In many cases they appear to have missed out on a normal childhood and adolescence and have been propelled too soon into the adult world. This may have the result of making them awkward socially as they no longer have anything in common with children of their own age but are not mature enough to blend in with others of an equivalent ability who are probably considerably older than they are.

Perhaps the most valuable of the talents to be brought forward from a former life into this one is the talent to be wise. Many families can cite cases where one child shows far more maturity than his or her siblings, almost from the beginning of life. Not only does such an attitude serve the individual well, both as a child and then throughout life, but it does not seem to prevent him or her from having a normal childhood with all the fun and enjoyment we would wish for our children.

It is believed by many – and indeed regression to various past lives would seem to indicate that it is so – that these 'old souls' probably will not have to return to life as we know it many more times in the future – if at all. They seem to have learned the necessary lessons of the spirit, making their mistakes in previous lives and just completing the final stages in their current one.

This does not mean, of course, that their journey of evolvement is complete – merely that they may not have to live on earth many more times. It is generally accepted that the learning experience continues in another dimension but, as yet, we have not been granted an insight into that other dimension.

LOOKING AT FUTURE LIVES

We sometimes hear of therapists who claim to be able to 'progress' people so that they may experience some of their future lives as well as their past ones. But among those who spend a great deal of time working with regression, it is not generally believed that this is possible. If, as is usually accepted, there is no such thing as absolute predestination, it follows that no one can know whether a particular spirit has learned the lessons chosen for this lifetime until this life is over. Since that is the fact upon which the lessons of the next lifetime are selected, it cannot be possible to look into that life until after the end of this one.

MOMENTS OF SIGNIFICANCE

Many subjects are asked, during the course of a past-life regression, to take special note of the most significant moments of the life they are experiencing. Once the regression is over, this moment will often form the basis of enlightening conversation between the subject and the hypnotherapist.

AVOIDING FALSE MEMORIES

When asking someone to note that which was a moment of significance in a former life, great care must be taken not to 'feed' them with information on a particular topic or period on which they should concentrate. This could easily lead to doubt about what really happened as well as about what should be learned from it.

A careful therapist will wait until the regression is almost over – even waiting until after the death experience, if this is to take place – before asking the subject to think back through that life and hold on to the thought or image of its most significant moment.

Some people find this quite difficult and might even ask for further guidance as to which part of that former life they should think about. The therapist has to insist that they follow their own intuition and decide upon a point that seems to them to have particular significance – even if, at the moment, they are not quite certain what that significance might be.

The word 'significant' has been carefully chosen as it indicates neither good nor bad and leaves the actual event and subject matter to the subconscious mind of the person being regressed.

The previous life being examined may not have been of great significance in itself – indeed the majority of them are not. But, however ordinary and uneventful that life may seem from the distance of time, there are bound to have been moments in it that had a profound effect upon the person living it. It is one of these moments we are looking for.

Sometimes the subject will spontaneously report a moment that he or she considers significant and then, having had time to think about it, will state that they fail to recognize what that significance might be. This does not matter at all; the fact that it came spontaneously to mind makes this a moment of importance and one worthy of consideration during the discussion that always follows a past-life regression.

For example, one woman stated that her significant moment was as an elderly man who was being treated kindly but patronizingly – albeit unwittingly – by his nephews. Shortly after this woman's regression ended, she claimed to have realized that her current attitude towards her ailing mother was precisely the same as the attitude she had so resented in her former life. This made her determined to change her behaviour towards her mother in this lifetime – and another lesson was learned.

A man who was a fisherman in a former life spoke of being blinded in an accident. It was quite understandable that this was a significant moment in that it changed his whole life from that moment on. No longer was he able to continue his work as a fisherman; no longer was he the provider for his family. In that earlier life it had turned him into a bitter and unhappy man for several years until he was able to come to terms with what had happened.

One might have thought that the significance in this life would be to place proper value on his eyesight – but that was not how the subject saw it. There were two lessons he felt he had learned in that previous lifetime and which, so far, he seemed to have forgotten in this one. The first was to appreciate all his senses – even as a blind man he had been able to feel the salt spray on his cheeks, the wind in his hair, and to hear the sound of the waves breaking and the seabirds calling. The second lesson was to allow others to care for him. In this lifetime he was a big man physically and took great pride in looking after his wife and daughter – yet he had failed to pay them the compliment of allowing them to care for him in return.

So, although the events deemed by the subject to be significant and the link between those events and their current life might not be what one would expect, the fact remains that examination of the 'significant moment' can prove a very valuable therapeutic part of the regression process.

EMPATHY

Experiencing past-life regression helps you to understand yourself more than you have ever done before, so it is also helpful when it comes to empathizing with and understanding other people in general – and those with whom you have strong links in particular.

It is not unusual for members of the same family – or particularly good friends – to discover more about themselves by regressing to past lives in order to understand each other on a deeper level. These regressions would not be carried out in a group situation. Instead, each person would have one or more individual sessions.

This would apply only to adult members of the family as those under the age of sixteen would only be regressed in very special circumstances (see the case of Ian, aged fifteen, on page 153). Although young children make excellent hypnotic subjects, it is generally thought that, even though they might easily regress into a past life, they do not have the maturity to cope with whatever they might discover during the experience.

As we have already seen, it is usual for those closest to us in one life to be very close in others – albeit in differing circumstances – so it can be extremely helpful to look at these relationships in detail in order to improve our understanding of our current lives.

Perhaps the relationship in a past life was an especially good one and this is being carried over into current times. Perhaps in a former life one person was extremely protective of the other and it now appears that the roles are being reversed. Alternatively, perhaps a previous life ended with unresolved difficulties between the two that could help to explain any current friction between them.

Although hypnotherapists do not set themselves up as marriage guidance counsellors, it is not unusual that couples who have experienced individual past-life regressions should then go together to the therapist to discuss what arose and what bearings those events might have on their current relationship. In such cases it is not the hypnotherapist's role to draw conclusions or to give advice but to act in a counselling capacity, giving each partner the freedom and opportunity to put his or her side of the story as they see it.

GENERAL UNDERSTANDING

Studying your own past lives does not only give you insight into those relationships that are currently closest to you but also helps you to empathize with people in general. Whatever an individual's beliefs at the outset of this journey of discovery, experiencing regression can only help when it comes to understanding the progression of the spirit throughout the lives examined. Once we realize that we are taking part in this great learning process, it must appear obvious that others are doing the same thing. And, just as children make mistakes in order to learn as they go from class to class in school, we begin to understand that mistakes made in this lifetime are all part of that same learning process. This, in turn, should help us to show more sympathy for the difficulties being experienced by others and to forgive some of the wrongs done to us – or at least to understand how they came about.

SPIRITUAL PROGRESS IS NOT AN EXCUSE

It is not being suggested here that anyone should use problems in former lives as an excuse for current bad behaviour or attitudes. Regression should be used as a diagnostic tool, enabling us to understand the cause of current problems – but it is then up to each of us to do something about improving the situation.

Similarly, although we may come to understand wrongdoers – and perhaps even forgive them – if the current human beings concerned do nothing to change themselves or their attitude, they are probably best avoided. All adults have the ability to change themselves, should they wish to do so. This may involve personal soul-searching or it may require professional help – but it is always possible. Those who do not make any attempt to change what they know to be negative attitudes or behaviour are failing to learn the lessons with which they have been presented in this lifetime. Of course, they have every right to ignore these lessons and to continue in the same old way – but it only means that they will have to come back and face the same lessons all over again in a future life.

Even those people who seek past-life regression out of what they consider to be 'simple curiosity' may find that their lives, beliefs and attitudes are changed irrevocably by the process.

[X]

A TYPICAL CASE –
STEP BY STEP

Not all of those who seek help from hypnotherapists to overcome specific problems will end up by being regressed to a past life. In some cases it simply is not necessary; in others the person concerned may feel uneasy about the process and would prefer to receive help in other ways. Sometimes, however, the regression will follow the suggestion of the therapist and the consent of the patient. What follows is a typical example of such a case.

THE PRESENTING PROBLEM

When Rachel first decided to consult me it was because she was due to go on holiday soon but was afraid of flying. At least, that was what she thought the problem was.

Whenever a patient expresses a fear of flying, the therapist will seek to discover which aspect of flying it is that causes this fear. For one person it could be the dread that the aeroplane might crash. This is probably the least common reason offered, as most people realize that statistics show they are far more likely to have an accident while travelling in a car than when flying. Some might hate the fact that they have no control over the situation when flying but are completely at the mercy of events. For others – and this was so in Rachel's case – the real problem was that they are claustrophobic and there are few places more likely to induce a feeling of panic in such people than the interior of an aeroplane – however large it might be – some thirty thousand feet above the ground.

A good hypnotherapist will always spend some time during the first consultation taking a detailed history from the patient. This often enables that therapist – as in Rachel's case – to see beyond what the patient believes to be the problem. Although there seemed to be comparatively few occasions during the course of Rachel's everyday life when her claustrophobia had the opportunity to reveal itself, she did mention that she also felt uncomfortable in lifts – although she used them when necessary – and she preferred to sleep with the bedroom curtains open.

DEGREES OF FEAR

Despite her fears, Rachel had travelled by air in the past – usually relying on alcohol to help reduce her sense of panic. But, as is the case with every phobia, the dread of flying was increasing and she had now reached the stage where she found it difficult even to contemplate making such a journey. This caused her great distress, not only because of her forthcoming holiday but also because she had a sister living in the United States of whom she was very fond. Unless she was willing to fly, Rachel was unlikely to be able to visit her sister in the foreseeable future.

THE PROGRESS OF A PHOBIA

Any phobia that is not treated will always get worse because each time sufferers tell themselves that the fear exists, they are reinforcing it and giving it increased importance in their subconscious mind. So what starts out as a minor nuisance can, if left untreated, develop into a crippling fear that affects many aspects of the patient's life.

WHETHER TO SEEK THE CAUSE OF A PHOBIA

In some cases it is essential to search for the root cause of a current phobia if there is to be any chance at all of curing it. This applies particularly to those fears that seem to have no foundation in logic. There are people, for example, who have a terror of butterflies, yet not only do most people find them beautiful, but there is no way in which a butterfly is going to hurt them. Others may suffer from a fear of a particular word or of the number thirteen; once again, there is no way in which the feared word or number can cause harm. In such cases, patients not only have to suffer the panic induced by the phobia but also the sense of shame or of foolishness that accompanies any fear without a rational explanation. These are the types of cases that always benefit from discovery of the initial cause of the problem.

CHOICE OF THE INDIVIDUAL

Many of the more common phobias do not require any sort of regression – past or present life – in order to help patients overcome them. At such times the hypnotherapist often asks patients to decide whether or not they feel the need to discover the original cause of the phobia. If they say that they do not think it necessary, it is quite possible to go ahead and help them to overcome their fear in three or four sessions.

On the other hand, if patients feel that it is an essential part of their cure to understand precisely how and why the phobia arose in the first place, the hypnotherapist will go along with their wishes and will seek to help them discover the cause. Rachel was such a patient. She felt that she would not be satisfied unless she understood exactly how her fears had begun.

RACHEL

As we follow Rachel's case, it is possible to see how a careful taking of history at the outset, plus a discussion with the patient, enables both patient and therapist to understand that the presenting problem is sometimes only a symptom of a deeper underlying issue. Having reached that conclusion — and, in this instance, because Rachel was determined to discover the cause of her claustropobia — it was necessary to proceed to hypnoanalysis.

EXAMINING THE CURRENT LIFE

Hypnoanalysis involves taking patients back by stages through the earlier periods of their current life. It is very important that this is done carefully and sympathetically in order to avoid any possibility of causing the patient distress. There is no point, for example, in saying to someone who is, say, twenty-eight years old, 'Go back to when you were twenty-seven... twenty-six... twenty-five... twenty-four... and so on. For one thing, this is too left-brained (or logical) a method and does not allow the patient to relax sufficiently for the subconscious mind to play its full role. For another, no one knows at the outset when some deeply traumatic incident may have occurred and it would not be good to suddenly thrust her into the middle of such a situation without any prior preparation.

A PLEASANT THOUGHT

When taking patients back to an earlier period in their current life, the hypnotherapist begins by asking them to think of something they found enjoyable when they were younger, or something that gave them comfort. Quite often this will be a memory of a happy family holiday, a favourite toy or a best friend at school. Even those who come from pitiable backgrounds and whose childhood was far from happy usually had a toy or a hidey-hole, for example, that gave them comfort, and so the hypnotherapist would begin with this.

THE HYPNOANALYSIS PROCESS

Having already explained the detachment technique to the patient and discussed how it should be used, the hypnotherapist will ask him or her to concentrate on the chosen pleasant thought as the trance is induced.

Rachel's pleasant thought was a memory of a birthday party when she was thirteen years old. It had been her first 'grown up' party in that it had been held in the evening instead of the afternoon, they had played records and cassettes instead of party games, and there had been a buffet of little savoury items instead of the usual sandwiches and jelly.

Using this as a starting point, I asked Rachel to think of the time immediately before and immediately after that party. I wanted to discover whether there were any situations that caused her fear at that time. Rachel was able to tell me that, even at that time, she did not like to sleep with the bedroom door closed and was uneasy about going into lifts.

By asking open-ended questions, I gave Rachel the opportunity to build up the picture of her life at the age of twelve to thirteen years. We then went backwards to incidents selected by Rachel's subconscious mind that revealed more about her earlier life.

THE SEARCH FOR TRAUMA

By this stage in the process, patients are usually so relaxed and so engrossed in the images of their early life that they forget what they are seeking. They are re-living or observing times that their conscious mind may have long since forgotten. Any therapist will be ever-watchful so that the patient can be gently reminded of the detachment technique, should this appear to be necessary.

Rachel rather enjoyed the experience of age regression. She had been the eldest of three children in a loving family and, apart from the usual minor tribulations of childhood, had no really bad memories to look back upon.

Even those incidents that demonstrated her early dislike of being in small, enclosed spaces were not too distressing as, in those long distant days, the dislike had not had a chance to escalate into the fear that it later became.

Having discovered that, even as a tiny child, Rachel had not been happy to be left alone in a room with the door shut and would not play with her young sister and brother in their tent in the garden, it became apparent that this dislike of enclosed spaces was something she had been experiencing for the whole of her current life.

THE DECISION TO EXAMINE RACHEL'S PAST LIFE

I asked Rachel how she felt about the concept of past lives and the possibility that the basic cause of her current problem lay somewhere in a previous incarnation. Never having contemplated this before, Rachel said that she did not know what she believed but was quite open-minded about the subject and quite willing to try past-life regression.

ALLOWING THE SUBCONSCIOUS FREE CHOICE

When taking patients through a past life experience it is never the hypnotherapist's place to instruct them to go to a particular previous life. In fact, this would be extremely difficult to do, as many have discovered. Nor is it possible to say that the immediate past life should be examined first, to be followed by the one before that... and so on. It is always left to the patient's subconscious mind to select the life it wishes to examine at any time.

The therapist will not take a patient back year by year in this lifetime, but allows the person's subconscious mind to choose which incarnation it is to consider. As with the current life, if this were not done, there would be the possibility of suddenly entering a past life at a stage where something terrible was happening – something with which the patient was as yet unable to cope.

When individuals seek past-life regression out of curiosity rather than to solve a problem, they often feel that there is a particular time in history to which they feel drawn or which has always fascinated them. Even in cases such as these, the hypnotherapist deliberately leaves the life to be touched upon open to be selected by that person's subconscious. In many cases, because that era is at the forefront of the subject's mind, it will indeed be the one to be selected.

Sometimes, however, the events of that particular life would be too traumatic for subjects to deal with during their first regression session. Even though individuals may be willing – indeed often eager – to examine their past lives, there is still a certain amount of apprehension about the process. In such cases the subconscious mind usually selects a life that was quite mundane and comparatively uneventful.

NOT ALWAYS 'FIRST TIME LUCKY'

It would be gratifying to think that the solution to a current problem would dramatically reveal itself on the very first occasion that a past life is examined. This is not always the case.

Occasionally – very occasionally – one past-life regression is all that is needed when searching for the cause of a problem in this lifetime but, more often, it may take two, or even three attempts. This is quite understandable because, if the original trauma was great enough to set up the ensuing problem, it is quite logical that the protective subconscious will initially avoid looking at it in great depth.

RACHEL'S LIFE AS A FARMER

Rachel's first past-life regression revealed that she had been a farmer in southern England at the turn of the twentieth century. It had been a comparatively hard life with just enough money for the farmer to keep himself, his wife and his children. Nevertheless he had been a happy and contented man.

This farmer had been the son of a shepherd and, from a very early age, would accompany his father to the fields to help tend the flock. He did not have much in the way of education but grew into an intelligent young man who, by hard work and diligence, managed to acquire a few acres of land and some livestock of his own.

In response to gentle questioning from me, Rachel examined various stages of this agricultural existence. The farmer had lived to a good age and had passed the farm on to his son, having the pleasure of seeing him tend the land and the animals with as much love and care as he had done.

What seemed to be significant throughout the whole of that life was that, man and boy, the farmer had felt the need to be outside in the open air, whatever the elements. He would return to their small house to eat and sleep but never felt entirely happy indoors.

This seemed to indicate that Rachel's claustrophobia had already been in place – although in a considerably milder form – during that earlier life and that it would be necessary for us to examine another life in order to see whether its cause could be determined. As it is not possible to predispose patients to go back through their lives in reverse chronological order, we could not be certain that the reason for Rachel's problem would present itself on this second occasion – although we hoped that it would.

THE HELPFUL SUBCONSCIOUS

In theory, it could take any number of sessions of past-life regression before the true cause of a particular phobia is uncovered – but this very rarely happens. Sometimes the explanation becomes obvious during the very first session but, in many cases, this is not so. The reason for this is that the patient is probably experiencing past-life regression for the first time and may be feeling a little apprehensive – which could be sufficient to cause a certain amount of tension and reduce the likelihood of going straight back to a traumatic event.

By the time of the second regression, however, the patient knows what to expect and – hopefully – trusts both the hypnotherapist and the technique. The subconscious mind of the patient is well aware of the reason for the regression and is likely to do its best to be helpful and lead him or her to the original cause of the current problem, so it is not unusual for it to become apparent during that second session.

RACHEL'S LIFE AS A MINER

This time Rachel regressed to her life as a miner called Jethro, who worked in a north-country coal mine. The work was hard, the pay meagre and the living conditions poor and yet this miner really liked his work. He got satisfaction from the results of his efforts and he enjoyed the company and comradeship of his fellow miners. He had a good wife and three sons and, despite being poor, they were a close-knit and caring family.

During the regression, I asked this miner whether he had ever thought of doing other work. The response was an adamant 'no'. There was little work around that was not connected with the mine, although there were jobs to be had at the pit face rather than below ground. But his father had been a miner, as were his two brothers, and Jethro had never wanted to do anything else.

The interesting thing of course, as far as Rachel's condition was concerned, was that Jethro had no fear at all of being underground or of climbing up the narrow shaft that led to the surface. It was obvious, therefore, that whatever the cause of her later claustrophobia, it had not yet occurred. Then came the day of the disaster.

Accidents in the mines were by no means unheard of and every miner there knew of at least one person who had been injured or killed while working below ground. But Jethro himself had never been personally involved, although he had assisted with the rescue of colleagues who had been trapped in the past.

On the day in question, the men were coming to the end of their shift when they heard a terrible noise. Suddenly the mine was filled with choking coal dust. One of the huge timber supporting posts close to where Jethro was working collapsed and huge amounts of coal and rock began to fall on the miners. Jethro was cut and bruised but not seriously hurt. But, all around him, he could hear the screams and cries of his fellow miners as they lay critically injured. Then came the silence.

As Jethro looked around him, he could make out the half-buried bodies of some of his friends. Others were nowhere to be seen, lost for ever beneath solid mounds of blackened rock. Jethro was the only one left alive.

Jethro knew that the men on the surface would make every attempt possible to rescue their buried colleagues but, in his deep and silent isolation, he had no idea whether they were near to finding him. He still did not know as he took his last painful gasp of that foul, black air.

THE SAFETY OF THE REGRESSION

What had happened to Jethro was terrible and frightening, yet Rachel was at all times perfectly safe and quite calm. I reminded her of the detachment technique, so she was able to observe the events as they occurred and report on them without them having any more effect on her than the events in a film or television play.

INITIAL REACTION

The discovery of the original cause of a phobia or other problem is not sufficient of itself to effect a cure. It is still necessary for hypnotherapist and patient to go on together to eliminate the problem and prevent it recurring in the future.

After the regression to Jethro's life, Rachel's first reaction was that she now had a valid explanation for her claustrophobia. She could easily understand how anyone who had been through an experience such as Jethro's might become frightened of being shut in and not in control of the situation. She no longer felt that she was 'stupid' (her word) for having such fears when others around her did not.

THE THERAPY

Most phobias are treated in a similar fashion. Patients are asked to use their imagination to visualize a scene that in the past they had felt unable to cope with – but, when under hypnosis, they are asked to visualize themselves coping with it extremely well while feeling calm and relaxed. They will then practise until they can do this in reality. These imagined scenes get progressively more advanced with each session.

Although Rachel originally came to see me because of a fear of flying, it was obviously not practical to have her getting in and out of aeroplanes during treatment. After some discussion – and because the real cause was her claustrophobia – it was decided to use the cupboard under the stairs in Rachel's house.

In session one, Rachel was hypnotized, relaxed deeply and asked to imagine that she was standing in this cupboard with the light on and the door ajar. When she could do this satisfactorily in her imagination, I asked her to go home and to practise until she could do it in reality – but on no account was she to force herself to do more than she felt able to do. Two weeks later Rachel was back, having reached the stage where she could stand in that open cupboard with no problem at all.

The next session involved her imagining standing in that same cupboard while someone she trusted stood in the hallway outside. She was asked to pull the door towards her until it was as nearly closed as possible – knowing all the time that she could push it open whenever she wished and also that there was a supportive person present to help her should she need it. Another two weeks passed and then Rachel was back again, having been able to complete that task.

Now she was asked to repeat what she had done before but this time to turn out the light in the cupboard so that she was in complete darkness. While doing this she concentrated on her relaxation technique. She also had the benefit of knowing that her friend was standing just outside the cupboard door. This time it took only ten days for Rachel to come back and report that she now had no difficulty at all in doing what had been asked of her. She couldn't believe that she could now stand in a small dark cupboard with no light and with the door closed without feeling any sense of panic at all – but this was the case.

Visualization is a very powerful tool and, when combined with hypnosis and relaxation, it is almost always successful in the treatment of phobias. Each time the subconscious mind 'sees' the patient being successful, it assumes that the success was actual rather than imagined. If you have done something many times in the past, you will have no problem doing it again in the future. This means that phobias treated in this way do not return at some later date.

A HAPPY OUTCOME
Rachel was now able to go on holiday by air without any problem but, even better news was to come. Some months later, I received a letter from my delighted ex-patient enclosing a photograph of herself with her sister, which she had taken on a recent visit to Boston.

[XI]

CASE HISTORIES

The following four cases are taken from my own files and are set out here because they are of special interest. In each case the details are accurate but, naturally, the names of the people concerned have been changed.

CASE ONE — IAN

Ian was fifteen when his father first brought him to see me – which is a year younger than I would normally regress but I felt that this was a special case. In addition, I had the permission of his father as well as of Ian himself.

Background

The family came from south London and for the whole of his life Ian had suffered from what had been termed 'a communication problem'. This meant that, whenever he was asked a direct question, he was physically unable to respond – the muscles in his throat would visibly constrict and the words simply would not come, however hard he tried. He was not an unintelligent boy but, because of this problem, had gained the reputation at school of being stupid – both in the eyes of the teachers and of the other pupils. Also for years he had been teased by the other children and this had naturally served to make him withdraw even further into himself.

As is so often the case, Ian's father had brought him to see me as a 'last resort', having been to doctors, psychologists and psychiatrists all over the country in a desperate attempt to help his son.

Initial hypnosis

Ian was very willing to be hypnotized and turned out to be an extremely good subject. The first thing we noted was that, while under hypnosis, he could answer simple questions without any difficulty at all. This gave us all hope for the future.

The regressions

Nothing of any great significance became apparent on the first occasion that Ian was regressed to a past life. However, there was one point worthy of note. During that regression, Ian reported that he lived in Ireland in the early 1800s and it appeared that the person Ian was at that time had no difficulty at all in responding to any questions that I asked him.

The second time I regressed him, Ian told me that he was an American pilot in the second world war and that he died under interrogation in Nazi Germany. After that he would say nothing other than his name, rank and serial number.

I knew nothing of the American military so I wrote these details on a piece of paper that I later gave to Ian's father. He was able to check with the relevant authorities and it turned out that there had been a 32-year-old US pilot who had been described in military records as 'missing; presumed dead'. This pilot had the same name, rank and serial number that Ian had given me during the regression.

The conclusion

The unfortunate missing pilot had not been famous; his details were not written anywhere where they could have been seen and noted by a young boy from south London. But, if Ian was accurate about the way in which the poor man had died, it was quite understandable that he would find it extremely difficult to answer questions when born again in the late 1960s.

The follow-up

When the regression was over, Ian's first reaction was to burst into tears. But they were tears of relief, not of sorrow. Although Ian had never expressed the feeling to anyone, he had been frightened for years that the taunts at school were true – that he was 'mad', 'thick' or 'peculiar'. Now he understood that, although he had a problem, there was an underlying reason for it.

I would love to be able to write that this knowledge brought a complete and immediate change in Ian's life and that he was suddenly able to communicate as well as anyone else. This was not the case. But there were many changes, and all were for the better.

Ian left school as soon as he was able to. He had never been happy there and his learning had suffered as a result. Also, other people had categorized him as unteachable for so long that they would find it almost impossible to change their view of him now. For a short time he took mundane and uninspiring jobs – lifting boxes for a local delivery firm and stacking shelves in a supermarket, for example. Then he met Pam.

Pam ran a small wildlife sanctuary and Ian went there to help with the small animals. This benefited everyone. Ian was able to give to these helpless creatures all the love and tenderness that had been locked up inside him and he had the satisfaction of seeing their response to him. Pam, who was used to dealing with those who had problems in their life, was able to give Ian the time to develop and to begin to communicate with her as and when he felt ready. As the months passed, she too had the pleasure of seeing him respond.

Perhaps Ian will never be what the world calls 'normal'. He may always appear to be shy or diffident with people he does not know. But he was able to change from a deeply distressed and almost suicidal teenager into a gentle young man doing a worthwhile job in the company of people who had taken the time and trouble to understand him.

CASE TWO — LYNNE

Lynne was twenty-two years old when I first met her but she insisted on bringing her mother with her to the consultation. An intelligent and potentially attractive young woman, she was painfully thin, her arms and legs protruding like matchsticks from her pretty summer dress.

It had been thought at first that Lynne was anorexic, but the opinion of the many consultants and specialists she had already consulted was that this was not so. Rather, she suffered from a phobia about eating. She would experience hunger but, as soon as she went to put the food to her mouth, she was terrified of tasting it. She was desperate not only to be cured but to understand how and why her phobia had arisen.

Having used hypnoanalysis to see if the cause could be found at an earlier stage in her current life (which it could not), I then discussed the situation with both Lynne and her mother and it was decided between us to see if the reason for her condition could be found in a past life.

The regression

Lynne immediately regressed to a time when she was a man called Jacob living in the early part of the nineteenth century. Jacob appeared to be an evil character whose life was given up to criminal pursuits – most of them involving violence. In the beginning he had pursued these activities for financial gain but, as he grew older and had amassed a considerable amount of money, he seemed to enjoy inflicting pain for its own sake and was, in fact, responsible for several murders – some by poisoning and others by strangulation.

It was fascinating to watch Lynne as the story unfolded. One part of her – the part that was Jacob – delighted in his wickedness and his ability to escape detection. The other part was horrified at what was taking place.

During the regression, it transpired that Jacob was a grossly obese man, given to all the temptations of the flesh but, particularly, to eating and drinking to excess. Lynne (as Jacob) described to me her 'fat white hands', her 'enormous paunch' and her 'many chins'.

After the regression

When the session was over, Lynne expressed her disgust at Jacob and his character and also her distress to think that she could have been such a repulsive villain in a previous life. We discussed this at length and I explained to her that the person she is today bears no responsibility at all for behaviour in a previous life. In fact, we must all have been wicked or foolish at some time in the past or we would by now have progressed to a stage in our evolvement where we no longer needed to experience life here on earth. The fact that she found Jacob so repulsive was a sign that she had truly evolved and was obviously a far better person in her current life. Fortunately, once all this had been explained to her, Lynne was able to let go of any distress and guilt she might otherwise have felt.

Because of Lynne's experience as Jacob, it was not difficult to understand the link in her subconscious mind between gross obesity and evil. She had, of course, taken things a stage further and had become obsessive about being thin (as opposed to slim), as if to ensure that there was no way in which she could ever do physical harm to another person.

Somewhere deep in her subconscious mind, Lynne had felt that, should she ever allow herself to become overweight, she would develop evil tendencies. For this reason, although she had quite enjoyed her food as a small child, as she grew older she could not bear to see her body growing larger.

Follow-up treatment

Using a combination of hypnotherapy and counselling, I worked with Lynne in two ways over the following few weeks. Firstly, she had to learn to put the image of Jacob where it belonged – firmly in the distant past. Secondly, she needed to begin to see her own body realistically and to develop the desire to increase her weight for the sake of her physical and mental wellbeing.

Some might think it wrong to base a cure on treatment that involved the shedding of responsibility for the initial problem. However, I would suggest that, where that problem arose in a previous life, this is quite acceptable. Nothing can be done to change the person in the past – in this case Jacob – but it was important to help the person in the present – Lynne herself – to better physical and emotional health. By relegating Jacob to the past and out of her conscious and subconscious life, Lynne no longer had a reason for her obsession with thinness.

Obviously, the stages towards the cure have been over-simplified here. In fact, Lynne and I worked together over a period of four months, by the end of which time she was beginning to eat normally and put on weight. She would probably never be fat, but I had no doubt that she would go on to achieve a reasonable weight for her height and age.

CASE THREE — TRUDI AND ELEONORA

I had been practising past-life regression for almost twenty years before Trudi and Eleonora came along. For a large part of that time I had wanted to meet a pair of identical twins who would be willing to be regressed to former lives. I was interested to discover whether twins who were truly identical actually shared their former lives as a single person.

We hear and read of identical twins – even those who were separated at a very early age – who do the same things at the same time as they grow up. For example, they might have the same illnesses at the same time, marry partners who have similar jobs, give birth on the same day, or simply choose the same clothes to wear. Having met several sets of identical twins – both male and female – I have personal knowledge of the way in which they often speak together or finish each other's sentences.

However, I could never find a pair of identical twins who were both willing to be regressed. Perhaps they were anxious about what they would find out. Perhaps they felt that, if they had in fact shared a former existence, this would in some way belittle or cast doubt upon the two people they were today. But I never gave up looking. Then along came Trudi and Eleonora.

These two women were in their early forties when I first met them. Born in Austria, they had been brought to England by their parents when they were very young and so had grown up to seem as English as their friends and neighbours. Each had married an Englishman, each had a son and a daughter and, living only two streets away from one another, they saw or spoke on the telephone to each other every day.

They were intelligent and independent women. Their faces may have been 'carbon copies', with similar hairstyles and make-up, but they did not dress identically, although their tastes were similar. I approached them to ask them whether they would be willing to be regressed to past lives. It was something neither of them had ever considered before, but they were both quite intrigued and willing to see what happened.

The first regressions

As this was really a form of research rather than a way of discovering the root cause of a problem, I felt it was necessary that Trudi and Eleonora were regressed separately but on the same day, one after the other. I did not want them to have a chance to discuss their experiences of their past lives during the experiment in case, however unwittingly, one was able to influence the other.

Trudi was the more nervous of the two so she volunteered to be regressed first, as she thought she might become anxious if she had to sit and wait while her sister was regressed. Nevertheless, she proved to be an excellent subject and had no trouble in regressing swiftly to a life of comparative poverty in a village in Russia in the mid-1800s. This was a relatively uneventful life. The woman that Trudi had been at this time lived her normal lifespan, having married a farmer and brought up five children in a tiny home in a small village.

Next it was Eleonora's turn and you can imagine my excitement when, without having spoken to her sister and with no guidance from me, she immediately regressed to the same country and to the same time. However, the similarity stopped there. In her former life, Eleonora had been a priest living a fairly protected life in a Russian city, never marrying but carrying out those duties required of such a person.

Further regressions

By now Trudi and Eleonora were as fascinated by the whole thing as I was. Even though they had turned out to have two separate and quite different lives, how was it that they had each regressed spontaneously to the same part of the world during exactly the same period? Did this always happen with identical twins or was there some form of telepathy between them? We decided to keep trying, to see if we could find some answers.

I regressed Trudi and Eleonora on two further occasions. Each time they spontaneously went back to lives that had existed in the same country at the same time – firstly in Saxon England and then in France immediately before the Revolution. On each occasion the two had led entirely separate lives with no areas of similarity or overlap at all.

The result

I know that one cannot draw many conclusions from a single experiment but, if the case of Trudi and Eleonora was typical, it would seem that today's identical twins had lived past lives that were quite separate. The fact that they had lived at the same time and in the same place was understandable as, bearing in mind that people who are important to us in one lifetime tend to be important in another, who is going to be more important than someone who eventually shares your life as your identical twin?

CASE FOUR — RICHARD

Richard was a very unhappy man. On his first visit, he almost crept into my consulting room – as if he was apologizing for daring to be there. He sat on the edge of his chair, twisting his fingers together and staring at the ground. When he did look at me, his eyes were filled with tears.

The background

Richard told me that his life was not worth living as he considered himself a sorry person and of no value to anyone. He had worked in the same company for over fifteen years and had seen all those who had joined with him promoted more than once, while he had occupied the same lowly position he had held from the beginning. He was now far older than anyone else in his department and was aware that he was looked upon as a pathetic creature by the young people who surrounded him.

Things were no better at home. His wife and three teenage children had no more respect for him than his work colleagues. His wife had always been a strong person and Richard had found it easier to agree with whatever she wanted than to start an argument that he knew he was bound to lose.

It is understandable that a man in his late forties would not lightly contemplate quitting a regular job, but one might wonder why Richard remained in such a miserable marriage. The fact was that he had such a low opinion of himself he believed his wife and family were justified in the contempt they felt for him and so their treatment of him seemed to be right, in some strange way.

Hypnoanalysis

Taking Richard back to examine the early years of his life, we could not find a single time when he had been a positive and assertive individual. As a small boy he had been intimidated by his two older brothers who used threats and violence to force him to do all their chores for them. He was bullied at school and his parents were either unaware of the situation or did not care enough to do anything about it.

It became obvious that we needed to go back to a life before this one to discover the cause of Richard's problem. Desperate for any kind of help, Richard was only too eager to agree to this suggestion.

The regression

Richard was so tense, and so convinced that he would fail at this, just as he felt that he had failed at everything else he had tried, that he proved to be a very difficult subject to regress. In a perverse way, he was almost frightened to discover that there was a reason for his psychological condition because that would mean that he would have to make changes – and he did not know whether he would be able to do so.

I spent some time talking to Richard, reassuring him that, whatever we discovered, I would still go on to work with him to help him develop a more positive and confident persona.

Eventually I succeeded in regressing him and Richard immediately went to a time when he had led a miserable existence as a slave to a band of travelling people in seventeenth-century Europe. It seemed that he had been taken by these people when just a baby because he could not remember any other life. But he knew that he was not one of them – his hair and skin were fair and his eyes were blue, while they had dark eyes and hair the colour of ravens' wings.

As their slave, Richard (he did not seem to have a name in that past life) had been compelled to perform all the menial and unpleasant tasks but, although he felt hatred towards his captors, he had been so badly abused and so humiliated, that he did not dare to express it.

The session of regression was not a long one because the pitiful slave's life came to a miserable end while he was still a very young man. When the detachment technique is used, the subject does not feel any grief or pain at the ending of a former life. Indeed, in Richard's case the life had been so unhappy that he was quite glad to be able to leave it behind him and death came as a welcome release.

follow-up treatment

We had now discovered the reason for Richard's lack of self- esteem, but this did not, in itself, provide a cure. We now had to work together to help him develop some inner strength and confidence.

Invariably, this is quite a slow process as we have to start with quite minor successes and then build upon them. Richard was a patient of mine for over six months. But, by the end of that time, although he would never have an aggressive or forceful personality – nor would he want one, having been too often on the receiving end – he developed a quiet confidence that, over a period of time, helped him to make some necessary changes in his life.

CONCLUSION

Past-life regression, when conducted in a properly guided and ethical manner, can achieve a great deal. Whether one is dealing with traumatic problems of the past or a desire to improve life in the future, regression can be a very valuable tool. We are all influenced considerably by people we have known, events that have taken place or words that have been spoken, whether we realize it or not. Since a therapy exists that allows us to make use of our memories – however deeply hidden they may initially appear to be – it seems only sensible to take advantage of that therapy so that we can create for ourselves the happier and more fulfilling lives we all desire.

USEFUL ADDRESSES AND FURTHER READING

Finding a past-life regression specialist
Not all hypnotherapists practise past-life regression so, if you feel that this is the road you wish to go down, it is essential that you find one who does. The following addresses should be able to provide you with the name of such a therapist in your area.

In the united kingdom
The Hypnothink Foundation
PO Box 66
Gloucester
GL2 9YG

In the united states of America
The American Association of Professional Hypnotherapists
PO Box 29
Boones Mill
VA 24065

cassettes
It is possible to buy cassettes that claim to be able to help the listener experience past-life regression on his or her own. However, I firmly believe that it is unsafe for anyone to experience past-life regression unless in the presence of a trained and qualified therapist, so I would urge you to avoid such cassettes. Cassettes that are designed to help the listener become accustomed to hypnotherapy or that describe deep-relaxation techniques can prove extremely useful.

Further reading
Goldberg, Dr Bruce. *Past Lives, Future Lives* (Newcastle Publishing Co Inc),
Moody, Raymond A Jr. *Life After Life* (Bantam),
Moody, Raymond A Jr and Perry, Paul. *Life Before Life* (Macmillan),
Perkins, James S. *Experiencing Reincarnation* (Theosophical Publishing House),
Walker, Benjamin. *Masks of the Soul* (Aquarian Press),
Wambach, Helen. *Life Before Life* (Bantam),
Wambach, Helen. *Reliving Past Lives* (Hutchinson).

index